There is a lot of *control* in this story. The male stereotypes in our culture represent men as having the control and power, the special status and extra privileges and benefits of being male. Is this really the truth? Do men actually have all this power and control? Or is this power and control more like the emperor's clothes that are, in fact, not really there?

We believe the  are often puffed and _____ to make them appear _____ lerneath men are just _____ the illusion is intoxic_____ _____ to see through it.

This book is intended to introduce these issues and to burst the illusion that men are invulnerable and above needing help. We hope that AGAINST THE WALL will assist readers in looking for specific ways to help themselves, or the men in their lives.

AGAINST THE WALL

Men's Reality
in a Codependent Culture

Marshall Hardy, Ph.D.
John Hough, Ph.D

A Hazelden Book

BALLANTINE BOOKS • NEW YORK

Editor's note:

Hazelden Educational Materials offers a variety of information on chemical dependency and related areas. Our publications do not necessarily represent Hazelden's programs, nor do they officially speak for any Twelve Step organization.

Copyright © 1991 by the Hazelden Foundation

All rights reserved under International and Pan-American Copyright Conventions. Published in the United States of America by Ballantine Books, a division of Random House, Inc., New York, and simultaneously in Canada by Random House of Canada Limited, Toronto.

No portion of this publication may be reproduced in any manner without the written permission of the Hazelden Foundation.

Library of Congress Catalog Card Number: 91-71493

ISBN 0-345-37454-1

This edition published by arrangement with the Hazelden Foundation.

Manufactured in the United States of America

First Ballantine Books Edition: November 1991

Contents

Contents

Preface

Sexism, the belief that men are superior to women, is among the oldest institutions in our culture. Sexism has survived when other cultural institutions, other political systems, even entire peoples have perished. Its longevity testifies to how deeply gender beliefs are ingrained in the social fabric.

In keeping with the sexist bias in our culture, many more women than men are "diagnosed" as codependent. Men escape the negative effects of labeling that so plague women, but at the cost of not receiving the helping hand many of them desperately need.

We have seen revolutions in this country led by African-Americans, women, youth, and technology. Some things have changed, many things have not. A revolution led by men is now on the horizon. What changes will it bring?

We dedicate this book to those men who have heard the call and accepted the challenge to change. To change themselves. Not because women want them to or because it is the "right" thing to do. After all the personal reasons have been said, it comes down to: It's time. The use of gender-specific pronouns (he, his, him) throughout this book is intentional. All of the stories and examples used, except those noted as ours, have been assimilated from multiple sources. Any resemblance to a particular individual or historical event is entirely coincidental and unintentional. We hope and encourage our readers to "take what is useful and leave the rest."

—THE AUTHORS

The Emperor's Image

Many of us can remember the fairy tale from childhood about the emperor and his new clothes. The story, by Hans Christian Andersen, has been translated into different languages around the world. The story goes something like this . . . .

Once upon a time there was this emperor who loved nothing so much as his own image. He was always willing to divert time away from his duties and responsibilities to pay attention to his appearance and the impression it made on others. He valued the clothes he wore above any other part of his image. He fancied himself the best-dressed person with the best image in all his kingdom.

Everyone in the kingdom knew about his vanity but seemed not to care much. After all, everything in the kingdom worked well enough, and most people seemed content with their lives.

One day a couple of public relations—PR—men arrived in town. They announced to everyone that they were *the* best image merchants in the entire kingdom and could construct *the* most admirable image anyone could desire. Moreover, they claimed, anyone who even glimpsed one of their images would be so impressed with its perfection, its boldness, its power, that they would be moved to applaud and think good thoughts about its owner.

The PR men explained that the ability to really appreciate the craftsmanship of their images marked people as members of the most sophisticated group in society. In German these people were known as the "jung und pretentious" segment of society, otherwise known as the "juppies."

Further, the PR men warned, the only people who couldn't appreciate the quality of their images were those poor and unfortunate ones who were either too stupid or too foolish to know better. These people, the PR men said, should be dismissed from their jobs or at least made to wear signs on their backs that read "Dummy!"

When the emperor heard about this he immediately thought, *I should have one of those images; after all, I'm the emperor.* So he called for the PR men and decided to pay them handsomely for their very best image. "How else to really show everyone that I am among the best and the brightest, not one of the dumb and foolish?" he asked himself.

The image makers soon had a contract and a huge commission. They began work immediately, toiling day and night it seemed. They talked continuously about the new additions to this image and how this made it better than any they had done before.

Soon everyone was getting curious about the emperor's new image. Every conversation seemed to include questions about who had actually seen previews of *the image* and who hadn't. As time went on, more and more people were claiming to have seen the image and to have been very impressed. These people would typically go on about the fine details of the image, about how it used only the very best imported fabrics. Then they would boast about being on the "short list" to have their own image made.

Of course, many other people didn't believe they could ever afford such an image; they only dreamed about owning one and how different their life would be if they could.

Now, as it was, the PR men actually were making no image. Still, they busied themselves each day with great activity and showed every hospitality to all who inquired about their progress. They described their "image-in-progress" in great detail to these curious onlookers. And, casually at first, they dropped hints about the wretched home conditions or the traumatic early family life of those who had not appreciated the beauty of the image.

They quickly followed these hints with acknowledgments that previous visitors who had praised the image were obviously above average in breeding and taste. Soon they were pronouncing each new visitor in turn as the most "sophisticated" yet to view their work.

On it went, visitor after visitor, each leaving the PR men's shop with his nose a little higher in the air than when he had arrived. As time went on the PR men dropped their courtesy and began to greet new visitors with harrumphs and eyes rolled to the ceiling. This worked just as well as people were by now already believers. Having been made to feel inferior by contact with all those who had had their noses elevated earlier, these latecomers were far more interested in gaining membership in the "club" than in an honest viewing of *the image*.

When the time seemed right, the PR men announced they were finished and called upon the emperor. The emperor had earlier sent members of his court to view the "image-in-progress.'' That way, he thought, he had avoided the risk of being exposed a fool, or worse, too stupid to be emperor, if he should fail to truly appreciate its magnificence. Having heard the official reports as well as all the gossip, the emperor's nose was noticeably higher. Any fear of being embarrassed had left him when the two PR men presented their finished ''image'' to the royal court.

As if on cue, the entire court broke into a chorus of ''oh's'' and ''ah's'' and shouts of ''bravo'' as the PR men uncovered the freshly minted image before the emperor. The emperor, his nose tilted even higher in the air by the applause, could see even less of what was actually before him than before. He eagerly exchanged his current image for the new one.

With great pomp and circumstance the ceremony continued with a parade down the middle of Main Street before all the subjects of the kingdom. Another chorus of ''oh's'' and ''ah's'' was let out, led by the juppies along the street and echoed by all the wannabe's who stood behind them on the curbs.

But then, out of the crowd, a small voice was heard to say, ''He's got nothing on!'' This shocking revelation was passed through the crowd, and finally the emperor himself heard it. But he pretended not to, and continued marching down the street, his nose yet higher than before, as the juppies chanted their ''oh's'' and ''ah's'' even louder.

Introduction

This book is a weave of two differently hued but complementary strands of thinking about people. The first strand represents the development of a special focus on men and the traditional beliefs about masculinity that most of us grew up learning from our culture. The second strand represents the problems of dysfunctional families and, in particular, the problem of codependency. Taken together, these two strands of information produce a new cloth, a fresh perspective on the problems and process of recovery, one that has never been given the attention the authors feel it deserves. This new weave is about male codependency.

The current model of codependency as developed over the last several years is in large part based on a female frame of reference. The original ideas and theories about what defines codependency were derived from the earliest identified codependents: the wife or girlfriend of the male alcoholic. Of course, not all alcoholics are male. In *Gender and Stress,* Paul Cleary reports that the lifetime prevalence rates for alcoholism of men are between four and six times those of women. By reversing the arithmetic, there are four to six spouses of alcoholics that are female and potentially codependent for every male spouse. The female bias was never made explicit in these first writings. As the concept of codependency evolved, the female basis of the original theory became lost. In its place arose the assumption that codependency was the same for everyone, male or female.

What we have today is a basic or core theory about codependency that is assumed to apply equally well to both men and women. While it's very common for psychological concepts to be developed without checking the assumption of gender neutrality, the authors want to tackle this issue head-on. Is the experience of codependency the same for men as it is for women?

The Emperor's Image

The story of the emperor and his imaginary clothes is about how deceptive appearances can be for men. Cultural wisdom tells us that it is women who are primarily concerned with appearances. It is supposed to be "feminine" to spend time in front of the mirror. Maybe, and maybe not. Some men get caught up in the illusion of how brightly colored their masculinity can seem. Only an emperor could get away with such vanity. Yet many men like to think of themselves as emperors.

But it is not only the emperor who gets caught up in the subterfuge of appearances—everybody does. On this level, the story of "The Emperor's New Clothes" is about how important appearances are to the ordinary guy who is doing his job and minding his own business. We know about the appearances women put on. What are the appearances that men put on?

The emperor in the story is naked, but all the adults comply with the subterfuge that he is not. They fear being devalued, losing their jobs, or looking foolish. So they claim to see what they don't actually see and to appreciate what is not there.

There is a lot of *control* in this story. Stereotypes in our culture represent men as having the control and power, the special status and extra privileges and benefits of being male. Is this really true? Do men actually have all the power and control? Or is this power and control more like the imperial image that is, in fact, not really there? Isn't the moral of this story that the emperor is really a human being, just like you and me?

The many images of masculinity, often puffed up and proud, are draped over men like regal cloaks and make men appear to be more than they are. Underneath men are just men, male-type human beings. But the illusion is intoxicating. It is not easy to see through it. Men participate in this charade, as do women. Mothers and fathers have their parts as well. Television promotes this fantasy, while our pulp heroes take it to extremes. The truth is: The emperor has no clothes!

The bottom-line truth is that men are human beings, not emperors (or unfeeling robots or knights in shining armor). Men don't need the charade; men don't need the conspiracies of silence from women, alternating with applause and then condemnation. Nor do men need the competition with other men to see who can be the "best-dressed emperor." What is the value of being an emperor if the cost is losing access to the reality of everyday life?

Who This Book Is For

This book is about men, but it is for everyone. That includes women. It's for the man's man, the guy who on the outside is tough and in charge, yet on the inside is falling apart because his wife has started talking about therapy, apartment hunting, and divorce. It's for the soft male, the polite, apologetic, and even-tempered guy who is so afraid of offending someone that he keeps himself permanently under wraps. It's for men who grew up in intact, healthy families and for those whose family lives were marked by abuse, neglect, or conflict. On the inside all of these men are much the same—they are far more dependent on others to feel secure and whole than they would ever admit.

This book is also for the women who are involved with these men yet don't understand what's going on with them. These men are out of touch with their feelings. They are trying to live up to an ideal of how they, as men, should feel and act. And, most likely, many of these men harbor deep within themselves the notion that they are failing in life.

Few men realize how much of their lives are lived in pursuit of the values our culture has traditionally associated with masculinity. These values—a primary focus on work, logical thinking, and always being in emotional control—have many benefits to men and their families. When taken to extremes, this pursuit of traditional masculine values becomes a cage for feelings, a stranglehold on life itself. It keeps these men looking good in the face of the setbacks of everyday life, but only at the expense of driving their emotional life underground.

You Are What You Feel

The very basis of who men are as individuals, as human beings, is not what they *think* so much as how they *feel* about themselves. Without access to his feelings a man can't help but lose track of who he is, what his priorities are, and what is normal for him. He can become (or may remain) dependent on others, especially women, to provide the warm fuzzies of life. Or he does without. The same can be true of his connections to his kids, to his social network, to his wife or partner, and even to his own emotional health and vitality. He is dependent on some key female to an extent far beyond what is good and necessary.

Men often confuse emotional control with personal independence. They tend to believe that a well-oiled and functioning governor on feelings is the truest measure of real independence. Such men limit what they say, feel, or do in order to keep up the image of manly independence. With the woman on whom he is dependent, this guy will claim to be helping her out, giving advice, direction, or protection; and he is. Those are "men's jobs."

Does this work? A sure-fire test is to ask a woman who has been raised to pursue traditional feminine values what her ideal man is supposed to be like. But many women have been changing their minds about these things lately; the "traditional" man is no longer what these women want. The old life-style leaves women feeling hemmed in, restrained, controlled.

Whether a man's life-style is marked by being tough, domineering, and "independent," or soft, reasonable, and pleasing, control is a major factor. If men are supposed to be "in charge," how do they accomplish this unless they are in control? But control always ends up provoking re-sentments, withdrawal, and conflict. It also reinforces the emotional isolation of the controller.

Emotional isolation is like a hollow tree. It looks okay from the outside, but there is no substance to it. The emotionally isolated man is a guy with a strong exterior and no depth of personality. Where we might expect a rich inner life there is instead a lack of ability to deal with emotional issues. The result, for men as husbands and fathers in families, can be that the emotional issues, the personal and sensitive problems of life and love, are neglected or ignored—anything but truly shared. Or, these issues are raised behind their backs. The women get together and talk about their husbands' stress from work, about their kids' problems, about the frustrations of their marriage. It happens without the men, and it happens all the time. If the truth were told, men rely on these conspiracies of women; they need them. (Do women need them also?)

The consequence of not being involved with the important issues of life is that men can become psychologically divorced from all the people they really care about and whose support is vital. These same people need men to be supportive and caring in return. Men can become locked into roles that make it hard to ask for help when it is really needed. These roles deny men the opportunity to talk about important personal issues. They severely limit the range of feelings that can be safely expressed.

Feeling, unquestionably the most central and important aspect of human experience, is driven underground by the limitations of these roles. With it goes the natural vitality that is the hallmark of a healthy life-style. These are the basic conditions of everyday life for far too many men in

our culture. And we haven't even begun to discuss codependency yet.

The Goal Is Awareness

Or have we? Here are the basic conditions of codependency: to not talk about personal problems, to deny the
experience of basic human emotional need, to severely restrict the expression of feelings. *Don't talk, don't feel, don't
express.* These are the same rules most American males
grow up practicing in order to meet our culture's expectations of masculinity, the definition of what it is to be a male.
These are the social rules about what psychological qualities
are okay for a man to express. Many of these rules, left over
from a long-past age, still survive in our heads, even if we
are from an intact family. When you add the risk factors of
growing up in a dysfunctional family, you more than com-
pound the problems. They become lethal, as will be explained later.

There is a great mystery about men, among men and
women alike. One reason is that authentic masculinity remains almost invisible in our culture. This may sound paradoxical given that we generally consider our culture to be
patriarchal, favoring men over women exactly because of
their masculinity. If there is any truth to the saying, "It's
a man's world," how could there be any mystery about
men at all? This book is intended to examine one part of
the mystery of men, an area that has traditionally been
off-limits in our culture: *the emotional self-awareness of
men.*

This knowledge has been hard to define for most men.
This is true even for many male therapists who remain
adept at analyzing feelings, thinking about feelings, talk-

ing about feelings, everything but actually feeling their feelings. Our culture is beginning to provide some direction and support for those men who are seeking changes in their life. A good example is the work of Robert Bly, Michael Meade, and John Stokes. They, along with others, lead weekend workshops for men who are seeking a deeper experience of themselves. The development of men's centers in cities across the country is more evidence of the breadth of this change.

A dependable source of knowledge of the hearts of men can be found in the texts of the great religions of the world. This is especially true of the Biblical teachings of our Judeo-Christian heritage. The gradual loss of the natural spiritual dimension in men's lives can be explained, in part, as a consequence of the culture's rule separating men from their emotions. After all, if you can't tell how you feel from what you think, how can you be sure of the presence of God in your life? Has anyone ever "thought" their way to God?

The spiritual dimension of life is about being able to be passionate about God. The ability to be passionate extends to having deep feelings about injustice, about your wife, maybe even about your work. Ultimately, being passionate is about being truly alive, happy, and content. It's about being centered in the experience of true self, self without illusions.

The heart, symbolically the seat of our feelings, is the gateway to our authentic self. We call this denial of feeling in men the loss of heart. A recovery of heart, a loosening and opening up of the door to emotional life, is what men, especially men who appear codependent, have most to gain on their path to recovery.

As a reader, whether you are male or female, this is likely to be the first book you've read on how codependency affects men and their relationships. You may need some degree of healing yourself, or will think of someone you believe needs help. This book is intended as an introduction to the issues and only a small step in that direction. *Our goal is to burst the illusion that men are invulnerable and above needing help.*

Personal, in-depth healing often requires the assistance, guidance, and support of professional helpers. Attendance in, participation with, and commitment to a self-help group is often a useful adjunct or alternative to therapy. We hope that readers will take the next step and begin looking for specific ways to help themselves or the men in their lives who need it.

Men have been much less likely than women to ask for help, be it physical, emotional, or spiritual. One consequence is that many men do not know whom to call or what exactly to ask for if they do call. From our experience of working with men struggling to recover from codependency and the depression and chemical abuse that often accompany it, we know that each man benefits from the process of self-discovery in his own way.

It is important to become familiar with the community resources available to you. Resources that you can find in many communities include therapists who specialize in working with men, men's issues groups, Co-Dependents Anonymous (CoDA), and Adult Children of Alcoholics groups (ACoA). Give yourself a chance to check out a therapist or self-help group for a while before you decide whether or not these resources are meeting your needs.

It remains a revolutionary act for a man to stand up and admit he cannot handle everything by himself! Many men will not have the courage to accept a revolution in their lives. But many men will. Hallelujah, the emperor is naked!

The Path to Wholeness

The authors believe that most men in American culture grow into adulthood unconsciously committed to the emperor image. This is the traditional training in masculinity that our culture offers. Women know that men are committed to this image, even if they don't always understand why so many men honor it.

Men often struggle for years without realizing how strong this commitment is within themselves. This awareness often develops from a feeling that in growing up there wasn't as much love, care, or real one-to-one time with our fathers as we needed. There is anger in many sons about this, stemming from a sense of being abandoned, ignored, or somehow unworthy of our father's time. The result is a feeling of having grown up too much on one's own, without the guidance, support, and education about life that we needed.

Later on, many men discover that their anger has mellowed, only to have a sense of sadness or disappointment take its place. Frequently, this stage in the process of healing is spurred by the discovery that we got more from our fathers than they did from their fathers. That knowledge lessens the anger at our fathers and awakens a sense of shared loss with them.

At this point all the great losses men have suffered over the millennia may come forward into consciousness: the loss of nature to life in the city, the loss of spirit to the war in Vietnam, the loss of community to the inescapable need to compete in corporate America. Is there any end to the list? Robert Bly talks about "the grief that has no name," a grief that is found deep in the soul of everyman. Recovery is a lifelong process that carries the opportunity for healing the deeper wounds in men's souls.

Where this process begins is with the anguish of men who grow up without a model of what it is to be a male who can both think and feel. Without this model many men find they are always searching for but never finding a sense of wholeness in their lives. The problem is that they most often look outside themselves for the missing piece.

They often find the missing piece in the heart-center of women. What men need is to reconnect with their own hearts, their own center of feeling. It's important to disentangle all the complicated compromises that men have made with life in order to not feel the bumps and bruises that go along with being a heart-centered human being. This is even more true if the pain is rooted in a history of abuse, neglect, and abandonment. Men aren't supposed to be victims, but they often are. The little boy inside has been hurt, and he reacts by hiding. Such a man's life will be burdened by the legacy of having grown up in a dysfunctional family as well as in a dysfunctional culture.

Men, however, need something more. They need to reconnect with the deep well of masculine spirit and energy that exists in everyman. Disconnected, the well is the source of the hollowness found in the grief Bly discusses. It is not simple. Without access to the well, a man must choose between being lost and vulnerable to the winds that blow through his life or steeling himself against those winds. If he chooses to steel himself against pain he will end up cut off from life. Unable to nurture himself, he has little option but to seek dependence on women for their nurturance.

But if he finds the well, he has an anchor placed firmly in the solid ground of authentic masculinity and the community of men. He has a positive image of what it is to be male, emotional, vibrant, alive, and whole. This is true independence.

PART ONE

Loss of Heart

No man is an island, entire of himself; every man is a piece of the continent, a part of the main.

—John Donne

What is it to be a man in today's world? What does it mean to be a husband, a father, a worker, a buddy? What is it like for men who have come of age during the last thirty years of the women's movement? Difficult questions made much more so by the fact that they are so new to our consciousness. Men have more options today, just as do women. Many of us remember singer Bob Dylan's line from the early sixties, "The times they are a-changin'." This is the beginning of the nineties, the twenty-first century is on the horizon, and the times are changing still. This book and especially this first section are not intended to answer these questions in all of their complexity. The aim of this section is to take a critical look at life from a man's perspective.

For far more than thirty years women have been arguing that they have been treated differently from men in ways that aren't right. They argue that there is a powerful yet hidden bias against women in favor of men. This prejudice is called "patriarchy." It works in our culture to exaggerate the qualities of men and discount the abilities of women. There is no question that women are right on this.

The relationship of men to women is the basic building block of society and culture. It is the foundation of the family. In a truly egalitarian society, men and women would face each other as equals. Different, but equal. Women's ability to bear children and men's large muscle mass are part of what makes them different, but not necessarily unequal. Hammers are not very good at cutting firewood. Yet no one would claim this makes saws intrinsically superior to hammers. Each has its own range of capabilities and limitations. So it is with men and women. Together they can handle most circumstances.

Biology doesn't make any rules about what a person can do with his body, it simply gives him a body to do with it as he will. Biology leaves it up to individual men and women to decide what each will do. Somehow, the opportunities for living life became rigid and unequal in favor of men. A representation of equal and unequal relationships between men and women might look like this.

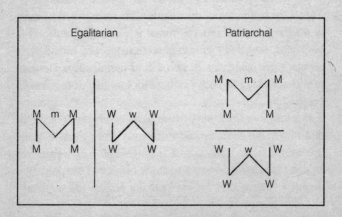

One result of the women's movement has been a host of laws and other precedents striving toward the economic, political, and social equality of women with men. While considerable attention has been given to women and women's rights, there has been very little attention paid to men and men's rights. A growing number of men and women now argue that men have also been mistreated by this same inequality. *The central theme of Part One of this book is that the dominant, patriarchal influence in our culture has as many rigid rules, roles, and stereotypes about men as it does about women.* The effects of these prejudices are as damaging to men as they are to women.

The idea that men should claim to suffer because of discrimination will appear new—even radical—to many. The authors don't intend to imply that every man will find himself completely characterized by the descriptions drawn here. The authors do believe that most men share a common heritage that is only in part a product of their unique natural families. The remaining influence is from the experiences of growing up male in a culture that has so many rigid rules and regulations about what it is to be a man.

As men grow up in this dominant culture, they tend to take these rules personally, so completely that they find it hard to tell where cultural values stop and their own values begin. Many men fail to find and keep happiness because of the strength of their unconscious commitment to the rules of masculinity laid down by our culture.

CHAPTER ONE

The Rules of Gender

Thinking versus Feeling

One of the new options men have in the nineties is to be whole and complete human beings. That means being tough, competitive, and logical. It also means being giving, vulnerable, and affectionate—in a word, *emotional*. It is not an either/or choice. It is possible for a human being to be both tough *and* emotional. Yet as men we have trouble with this. We believe that we must choose. We often pretend against all reason that we are okay when we're not, or that we can "handle it" all by ourselves when some help would be nice. We find it difficult to talk constructively about just those things that are most important to us: our marriages, our kids, our parents.

Bob had been referred to therapy the first time two and a half years ago, but today was his first meeting. He was feeling awkward and wanted to explain: "My boss just won't let up. . . . He keeps changing the rules on me. . . . The kids are pushing and pushing until I have to lay down the law." He didn't mention his wife or let on about his temper, the explosive outbursts at home and at work, or give many details about how "life has always been tough."

Earlier in this section, English poet John Donne reminded us that we are inexorably tied to one another. Most of us would agree with the statement that women find it easier (necessary?) to *feel* a part of a greater whole, whether this be their family or community or a group of female peers. The key word here is *feel*. Not just *think*, but *feel* themselves to be part of something greater than themselves.

The experience of emotion is like that. Feelings, especially positive feelings, tend to unite people, bring them together and hold them together, even over their individual differences. Feelings transcend individual differences by focusing attention on what is held in common. In this way, feelings tend to breed a sense of equality among people.

That's incredibly important. To truly feel an equal part of a group—openly, honestly, full-heartedly—with one's family or close friends is something special. The real contact, the felt closeness and acceptance, needs no explanation or qualification. Most of us know what this closeness is; we have experienced it.

But many of us have known too little of this joy, this unqualified acceptance. Many of us don't quite know how to give of these feelings either. And it seems men fall into this last category much more frequently than do women. How many sons can remember their father's love being expressed as criticism? "You got straight *B*s, how come no *A*s?" or "You got straight *A*s, how come you didn't get *A*s last time?" The criticism was intended to be helpful, not hurtful. How many generations has it been going on like this in our culture?

We have other feelings also. To feel that we are more

than or less than someone in our group leads directly to behavior, often subtly expressed, that puts us out of real contact with the people who make up the group. Envy, greed, and jealousy are examples of negative emotions that serve to undo all that the positive emotions create. What about feelings of competition, the desire to get ahead, to be in charge? Where do they fit? Is there a definition of competition that also allows for cooperation?

Limitations of Feeling

Feeling, like everything else, has limitations. Unchecked positive feeling tends to develop so much equality and togetherness that individual boundaries become blurred and lost. The classic example is the honeymoon couple, sitting in a restaurant booth, their eyes locked onto each other, oblivious to the repeated requests of the waitress or waiter for their order. This may be a pleasant experience for the honeymoon couple, yet this kind of behavior won't be very functional at the office. The "me" gets lost in the "we." It is hard to make decisions, to act responsibly, or to plan appropriately for the future if you only use feeling as your guide.

To choose feeling over thinking is not the answer. Women have traditionally been allowed a wider range of feeling than men, and it has not been enough to enable them to feel whole. Claiming the right to think as well as to feel is part of what the women's movement has been all about.

Men, by contrast, tend to value differences as opposed to communalities between individuals. Men stake out their personal identity as something special. Men want to claim the title of lord of the house, or at least chief of the tent.

Does this sound a little like an emperor, proudly strutting his new "image"?

Limitations of Thinking

Men in our culture are supposed to be more independent, logical, instrumental, and thinking than women. The key word here is *thinking*. The process of thinking is one of discovery, of discerning the differences between similar things as well as the similarities between different things. It is also about making judgments, about separating one thing from another based on criteria of which belongs where and why. The capacity to think involves the ability to make decisions and to plan for the unexpected. By focusing on our capacity to think, we develop the abilities necessary for managing conflict, performing math equations, and designing or fixing mechanical equipment. But has all this ability to think brought men any closer to full happiness than has the freedom to feel for women?

What's the problem here? Part of it is that men are generally reluctant to compromise their independence for the sake of having connections with others. Typically, women are just the opposite; they are too willing to surrender their independence for the sake of their connections to others. As men we pride ourselves on our independence perhaps more than any other characteristic.

Of course, we're not talking about actual behavior here. No, in the humdrum of the average day, we compromise quite a bit. Men are likely to wear the class tie and the work uniform. Men "belong" to many groups.

The problem is that many of us want to be seen as different, special, a cut above. This is the masculine ideal. We get so caught up in the pursuit of that image that we tend to forget that the connections to the mainland are what keep us afloat. And the mainland that really counts for us is not the office, but our friends and especially our family. We don't have to choose between self and relationship. There has to be another option. Why do so many men never find another option? What gets in the way?

The Rules of Masculinity

The basic rules of masculinity define the attitudes and characteristics that a man should value and strive for in his day-to-day relationships with others. The most important of these rules are expressed as ideals. A look in the dictionary reveals that *ideals* are "a conception of something in its perfection" and "a standard of perfection or excellence." By definition, ideals are the epitome, the highest standard, and the most important of values.

Who doesn't want to be the best? Masculine ideals are the qualities that our heroes rely on to slay the dragons, win the love of women, and gain the respect of their fellow men. These qualities include unflinching courage, resolute determination and perseverance, chivalry to women and children, honesty, intelligence, and loyalty. These are truly outstanding qualities. Where would we be if there weren't men (and women) with these qualities who were willing to fight the dragons of the world on our behalf, even at great risk to themselves?

In an age before computers, before blitzkrieg, before the advent of machines, physical prowess was also a critical quality for a man. In an age before nuclear fears and "the button,'' the only way to fight dragons was up close. The male advantages in physical strength, quickness, and stamina were crucial to defending home and family against foreign raiders as well as local outlaws. In a world that recognized no value separate from the sword, the stronger hand prevailed. In this way, men's identities were as firmly grounded in their bodies as were women's identities in childbirth and motherhood.

As much as men and women in this earlier age had in common, a rough division of labor had men in charge of the world outside the family while women continued their primary responsibilities inside the family. The world outside the family home was the world of potential danger. It was also the world of men. If there was danger threatening the family, it was from a band of marauding men. The thief in the night was most likely a man, as was the local entrepreneur who through foul means or fair was a necessary trading partner of the family.

A reading of a good history text will show that physical violence or the threat of violence was a daily companion to families of the premodern era on a scale much larger than anything we know today. We may need locked doors, but not walled cities. And it calls attention to the fact that the external world, the place of potential danger, of economic and political competition, was primarily a male domain.

The world has changed in many ways. Aside from Hollywood, the lone knight on horseback has no place. It is not likely that Minnesota will ever be overrun by barbarian hordes. Yet, other things have not changed. The physical violence in our society is still committed predominantly by males. It is still men who are the principal antagonists in the economic and political warfare of our time.

The external world is still dominated by men. Physical violence may no longer be as common as it once was, yet competition in less lethal forms is still a primary aspect of relationship between men.

Factories and the Family

The external world in our modern society is in large part the world of work. It's the rat race, the jungle, Madison Avenue, and Wall Street. To get a job, keep a job, get ahead, or plan for retirement, the external world is still a tough place to survive. To survive today, staying alive and well fed, requires the same qualities as an age ago. Or does it? The change from the life-styles and habits of the Old World to the customs and relationships of the modern hinges on the effects of the industrial revolution.

The industrial revolution changed the world in so many ways. What interests us here is how it profoundly affected the lives of men. The industrial revolution, more than anything else, is associated with the advent of machines. The rising importance of the factory, which was nothing but many machines organized into a functional unit, soon followed.

The key point is this: Before the advent of machines, men were seldom separated from their families. It was common for all the work necessary to keep a family sufficient in food, shelter, and comfort to be done by teams of family members. This may have involved groups of teams from different families. What was crucial was that men did what was considered men's work in the fields or forests with their older sons at their sides. Women had their own jobs, and they were helped by their daughters and young sons. Everyone might have come together to help in the big jobs, like harvesting the crops. Neither parent had to routinely spend long periods away and on his or her own without the personal contact from family members and the possibility for support that this proximity offered. Until the coming of factories.

With factories came the real breakdown of the family. It affected us all, not just men. But it affected men especially hard. Prior to the coming of factories, a son was likely to accompany his father throughout the workday. A son learned firsthand about how men handled the problems of life. He learned at his father's side how to deal with other men. He participated in his father's successes and failures. He got to see how his father handled conflict, how he co-operated with others. He got on-the-job training in how to be a man. And that included how a man handles his feelings.

With the advent of factories, fathers and sons, in increasing numbers, went off to separate jobs in different places. Women and their daughters did the same. Yet some differences remained for women. However the world might change, women then as now have to be present at the births of their children, if not longer. But fathers don't. And increasingly they didn't. Furthermore, the new commercial world developed barriers against the full participation of women, restricting them to jobs that were the lowest paying, the most routine, and the least prestigious.

In effect, men got a new option (or so it seemed): to go to work. Women got more of the same, only mechanized. As Warren Farrell has noted in *Why Men Are the Way They Are*, the new goal for women was to marry a husband who earned enough because, alone, she couldn't earn enough for herself and her children.

The other major event was the passage of child labor laws restricting the hours and conditions of labor for children. The effect of these laws was to return children to the home. Going to school became the child's new "job." What was once a system of job specialization along gender lines in an agrarian society became a system of job specialization geared to the needs of the factory, not the family, in an industrial society.

The Demands of Being a Worker

Women, for the most part, did not lose touch with their families in the way men did. But, the roles of father and husband increasingly took a backseat to the demands of being a worker. Increasingly, men were trained by our culture to focus on their ability to provide economically for their families. That was what counted.

Few work settings, jobs, or professions rewarded men for their emotional vitality. Thinking skills were valued and rewarded over emotional skills. In fact, feeling was seen as something that interfered with a good work attitude. It was taken as a sign of trouble. It marked the worker as being too personally involved with his life to be productive. A worker was supposed to leave his problems at home. That is, he was to check his feelings at the office door and pick them up again on the way home.

The model of men as workers, as straight-ahead, no-nonsense thinkers who focused on getting ahead and were cognizant of the dangers of competition became the dominant model. A man measured himself by his success at work. This left women alone with their children and the management of the home. The division of labor had become absolute. The meaning of fatherhood shifted from the active involvement of the male parent in his children's lives to a title that identified the seat of family authority. Little boys continued to take after father, "as they should," learning to repress, control, deny, and avoid their feelings. The idyllic 1950s family of "Father Knows Best" fame was in the making.

Our society has gained materially from this course of events. We have also paid a high price for this "progress." As for men, their newly found "option" to go to work soon became another casualty of the changing times. Going to work became an obligation. Again, as Warren Farrell notes, the new equation was:

No job = no wife, no job = no family, no job = no real happiness.

What about the values and ideals, the rules of masculinity—what happened to them? How have they evolved to keep pace with the changing world around us? The answer is they haven't. They are still very much with us, unchanged and increasingly out of step with the needs of men in the modern world.

Before the industrial revolution most of the average man's time was spent with family. Love, care, concern, support, discipline, and simple emotional availability are the key ideals for family matters. And they are ideals for everyone, not just men. Men didn't just become isolated from their families as much as they became absorbed by the work world. Insofar as corporate warfare has taken the place of actual warfare, corporate ethics have taken the place of personal ethics for many men. The ideals that were once meant to guide men in dealing with the true dragons of the world have come to represent a way of dealing with the world itself.

Masculinity and Codependency

It's good that things continue to change—if slowly. A number of recent studies show that men continue to define themselves and their self-worth in terms of their work, their ability to produce and compete with other men. To beat the other guy still takes precedence over simply being the best we can be. We expect it of ourselves. We expect it of our sons. Women still expect it of us as well.

But this ethic of always being ready to confront the dragons of the work world is counterproductive as soon as we cross the threshold of our home. The truth is, it's not humanly possible for men to check their feelings at the office door and then pick them up again on the way home. No one can turn their feelings on and off like that. The truth is, by the time young men are old enough to work they have already learned to simply check their feelings, period.

One of the most prominent ideals in our culture is that men are supposed to be strong enough, competent enough, and intelligent enough to handle their problems on their own. Especially emotional problems. This is the ideal—that real men are supposed to be ''independent.'' The test of independence is to not need anything or anyone to get by. If circumstances called for us to get along on our own, we could. We might even want to.

This is one of the most important of the rules of masculinity: Real men are independent of each other and everyone else. The Lone Ranger, the movie image of John Wayne, the Old Man and the Sea, are some of the incarnations of this rule that come immediately to mind. There are countless others.

All this concern about appearing independent is actually

about the need to prove oneself worthy of respect, love, and acceptance. It is also one of the biggest confusions men struggle to sort out in their lives. Men confuse being independent with being alone, separate, uncommunicative, silent.

Being alone is actually easy. The real challenge is to be independent and still be able to share with others. To be independent and close. Far too many men end up "independent" and divorced.

The form of this ideal that men live up to in public, usually expressed in a negative form, is: Don't wear your feelings on your sleeve. It means we are not supposed to let our deeper feelings show. Don't be too emotionally visible to others. It's better to be emotionally opaque than obvious. Of course, after years of practicing deceptions like this, we end up being the ones most confused and out of touch.

If you are familiar with the literature on codependency, you will remember that codependents typically end up identifying with those same injunctions. The point is, *males grow up with a rule in their heads that tells them to separate from their feeling and focus on their thinking*. And that is just what most men do; they separate their thinking from their feeling, their heads from their hearts, as a matter of course, codependent or not.

In fact, the codependent injunctions against talking, trusting, and feeling all have counterparts in the traditional rules of masculinity. The extreme male stereotype is of a guy who appears *always* sure of himself, *always* tough under pressure, and able to handle *any* problem on his own. He is also typically a guy who won't talk about personal issues, is too proud to trust anyone to really care for him, and keeps his feelings under close guard.

This connection between the rules of masculinity and codependency is important. Note the following definition of codependency by Robert Subby in his book *Lost in the Shuffle* (1984):

> An emotional, psychological, and behavioral condition that develops as a result of an individual's prolonged exposure to and practice of a set of oppressive rules, rules which prevent the open expression of feeling as well as the direct discussion of personal and inter-personal problems.

Caretaking: The "Feminine" Aspect of Codependency

Other definitions of codependency will be discussed later. The question here with Subby's definition is, what are we talking about, masculinity or codependency? It's hard to tell, isn't it? Yet masculinity and codependency are definitely different things, aren't they? Or maybe the problem is that codependency and femininity are mixed up? Or is it masculinity and femininity?

There is a traditional value in our culture that defines the expression of feeling and direct discussion of personal problems as the woman's responsibility in a relationship. It's one of the rules of femininity. A wife is the only one who is supposed to care for, look after, support, and, in general, nurture the emotional life of her family. It was once her exclusive job, and it included taking care of her alcoholic husband. That's part of the reason why it was so difficult for early researchers into alcoholism to realize she had a part in the family disease of alcoholism and needed help herself, even though she was doing what was expected of her! From her own values as a female, as well as the traditional values of middle America, she was being a good wife and acting "feminine" by continuing to nurture, caretake, and enable her alcoholic husband.

The reality was that these "responsibilities" were all too oppressive, eventually overwhelming and debilitating to her. The rigid and oppressive rules of behavior, thinking, and feeling that develop in families of alcoholics create the same kind of conflict that is experienced by women from intact families. The result was that women from all walks of life found their aspirations for autonomy and self-respect in conflict with their allegiances to the traditional values of their culture.

The struggles of so-called dysfunctional women can be seen as a microcosm of the struggle of women in general. What women from healthy, intact families as well as from alcoholic families did with this struggle was surprising to the entire culture: they rebelled! They began throwing off the burdens of a patriarchal culture, especially its discounting of feeling and of caretaking roles. They began to realize they were not the problem. They began to realize that the culture's expectation of them as women was the real problem.

The women's movement was created in the awareness of women across the country that it was the culture's problem and it was the culture that needed to change. By the "culture," many women really meant the "males." "It's not us; therefore, it must be them." The *concept* of codependency developed during this same period, although the word *codependency* was not actually used. Yet somehow the connection was never made that women were set up for codependency by their obedience to our culture's rules of femininity: to be loyal, nurturing, and forgiving caretakers of men.

The focus of the problem remains on the caretaking aspect of codependency, the "feminine" aspect of codependency. The connection between codependency and the rules of femininity has recently surfaced. Given this understanding of the connection between femininity and codependency, it is clear that codependency treatment for women is really about treating the pathological effects of discounting women. Where does that leave the issue of men and codependency?

The Challenge of Gender Awareness

Why are we spending so much time talking about women in a book about men? Because the struggle to bring a gender awareness before the public has been a challenge that women have worked on for two hundred or two thousand years now. Because gender awareness—awareness of the set of attitudes, beliefs, values, and habits of thinking, feeling, and behaving that define masculinity and femininity —is not just a woman's concern. Gender is not just a feminist issue. Women have been the leaders in this movement, and men need to acknowledge the debt they owe women for their courage and commitment.

The truth is, gender is something men "have" and value just as highly as do women. It is as important to men to be masculine as it is for women to be feminine. Men struggle with their allegiance to the rigid, arbitrary rules of masculinity just as women struggle with their allegiance to the rigid, arbitrary rules of femininity. Men suffer from sexist oppression in our culture just as do women. Comprehending this is crucial to a complete understanding of life problems from a man's perspective. These problems include being able to ask for help, giving in to someone else's opinion, coming home from work at a decent time, and allowing ourselves to feel. Sexism does, and always has, cut two ways.

CHAPTER TWO

The Secrets of Gender

Open Secrets

Open secrets are the most complex of secrets. They are the kind of secrets that (1) everybody knows about, and (2) everybody pretends he or she doesn't know anything about. An open secret is a little secret that everybody knows wrapped up in a larger secret that is really unknown.

The mystery of open secrets is about how little secrets can be known to us, yet still remain a secret. The mystery is also about how this can continue indefinitely, resisting change and trapping all those involved in a cloud of denial.

The emotional life of men continues to be one such secret. The little secret is that men exist on this planet as thinking and feeling human beings. They always have; we've just "forgotten" it. Men have all the same needs and all the same basic "wiring" as women. This secret we all know. Our personal experience of life tells us this. The larger secret is about how, in spite of this, we have conspired to keep the emotional life of men a secret. And it is a secret, just as the thinking life of women has been kept a secret for so long.

All men and women experience the painful side of these rules of masculinity and femininity in their lives. Yet the experience doesn't seem equal at all. Men somehow come out better than women, even if men have their own difficulties. The system of beliefs about gender has special rules that stipulate men are to be taller than their wives, make more money, pay less attention to their dress, drive the car if both are inside, and so on. Men, even in their disabilities, are to keep up the image, if not the reality, of being stronger, smarter, and more durable than women.

Somehow, it is still a "man's world." Fewer people today would support this belief than in years past. Yet everywhere we find people (ourselves!) acting as if they did. This very basic inequality seems to be at the very core of how our society is built.

Thanks to the women's movement we have become aware of the privileges our society grants men and the limitations it imposes on women. It is wrong that, as men, the abilities, advantages, and opportunities granted to us should come at the cost of the denial of these same benefits to women. We shouldn't want our happiness to depend on someone else's unhappiness. That is, in the end, debilitating for both sexes.

The ones who are denied equality of opportunity and free expression of their abilities are generally the ones who are first and most aware of that inequality. The experience of the inequality is painful and frustrating for those who get the short end of the stick. For those on the privileged end of things, the inequality acts like a narcotic, dulling the sense of the full experience, including the cost, of that privilege.

As men, we are largely unaware of the costs society levies on us for the exercise of our privilege. Men traditionally have had the obligation to get up at three in the morning to check out the noise downstairs, to take the risks of initiating intimate contact, to join the military and sometimes not come back. Many men continue to be the primary person responsible for the immediate and long-term financial security of their families.

We know about those costs; we even take a certain pride in them. By accepting these responsibilities we sometimes argue that we, as men, have earned our privileges and have a right to keep them. That is a rather common belief and a way of understanding the unequal allocation of costs and benefits in our society.

Another way of understanding this arrangement of costs and benefits is this: Masculine privilege is the mechanism men use to keep themselves emotionally safe. The chief benefit of masculine privilege is the option of being emotionally invulnerable. Women don't have this option of being emotionally safe. In a traditional culture women are forced to rely on men for their safety.

The problem is that the rules of masculinity turn this option into an obligation. Men have little choice about risking their emotional safety. There are a few rules that tell them when to risk and many rules that tell them not to risk. *Real men obey the rules.*

Real life doesn't follow the same rules that real men do. The result is that men are often in conflict with the feeling dimension to life. This is the primary cost to men for their privilege.

What we never seem to see clearly is that men suffer inordinate health costs associated with the stresses involved in maintaining their privilege. The statistics on population mortality show that one-half of all men will die a *minimum* of eight years before the average woman.

If you are reading this book in a public place, look around. Realize that every other man in your view will succumb to illness eight or more years before his wife. Where is the privilege in this?

So why haven't men taken the lead in demanding change beneficial to themselves? As the theme of this chapter suggests, there is something slippery about the subject. You have to be careful about putting the issues of men and feeling side by side. There is something immediately discomforting about such a picture.

Many people believe that women are biologically programmed for feeling and nurturance while men are programmed for mathematics and aggression. These people assume men and feelings go together only in extremes. Then you have a man who is either dangerous or pathetic. And there are those who believe that if you closely examine a man who appears to be feeling you will find that he's really thinking. That's amazing. How is it that in this society of advanced technology and sophisticated culture we maintain a myth about the abilities of men to fully experience life?

Are Men Different?

A myth, a secret? A secret about what? Beryl Benderly has investigated the evidence for a number of assumptions about gender in her book *The Myth of Two Minds*. She wonders if the actual biological or neurological givens of the male of this species are relatively less able to support the experience and expression of emotion than women, or if males are simply "wired" differently, and as a result are not tuned into the nuances of interpersonal give and take, that area of life which gives rise to much of what's emotionally important to us. Maybe it's possible that men really have become as strong and independent as they seem to claim, to the point of being invulnerable and unneeding of emotional contact.

She finds a number of groundless assumptions that pop up in scientific articles and cocktail conversations alike about how males are genetically or instinctually more aggressive, or that their brains can't "crosstalk" as well as females. The myth that men and women have little in common and much that is different is repeated by many people, scientists and laymen alike.

Yet if we were to accept the myth as true, then the obvious conclusion must be that women are the more culturally and psychologically advanced! Most of the so-called feminine traits are quite socially sophisticated, while many of the so-called masculine traits are crude and barbarian. Where women have been subordinated by a sexist ideology that describes them as the "weaker" sex, now men would be subordinated as the more primitive sex. Poor fellas, they just can't help themselves!

This issue of men and feelings is not so simple as this. Nor is it just a subterfuge about how men, in fact, do feel, but just don't admit it publicly. That is in part true; men are cagey about expressing their feelings. But this issue is different. This is about an open secret.

Taking Stock

Before going on, let's stop and take stock of what has been said so far. The authors have noticed time and again that a point occurs where a client turns a corner in his process of recovery and for the first time sees himself as a three-dimensional man. A man, not just a human being. A human being with specific gender. Human beings always have gender; there are *no* exceptions.

Many men seem to think, *Hmm . . . gender, everybody's got it. Where is my gender?* The first answer is sometimes, *Aha, it's right here in my pants!* No, those are your genitals. Gender does not mean sex. Gender is different. For both males and females, gender is two sets of attitudes, beliefs, values, and habits of *thinking, feeling,* and *behaving* that each succeeding generation hands down to the next. One set defines that which we call masculinity and the other femininity.

Ideas about gender vary from culture to culture and from time period to time period. Yet there remains a remarkable similarity across cultures and time. Gender is most clearly expressed in the pattern of complementary roles that develop in interpersonal relationships. A man's job, place, or style versus a woman's job, place, or style. Gender is a key piece of life's problems as well as part of any potential solution.

Men get to the point where they can actually see a pattern in the way they think, feel, and act. They see a pattern of subtle and sometimes not so subtle attitudes about what is right or wrong, manly or unmanly. They get the connections between their feelings of pain and regret and how they have chosen to live their lives. They remember some of the criticism they have been given: "You never listen" or "You always had to have it your way"—two of the most common examples. They see how they share with many other men a reliance on thinking and problem solving along with a real avoidance of expressing their feelings too deeply.

What's the big problem with expressing feeling? Well, one reason is that getting into feelings can seem like losing control, and that's definitely not manly.

That males have gender is one of those open secrets. We all know it, but we still walk around acting like we don't. If you look up gender in the dictionary, you can find a statement like, "sex: the feminine gender." That's it, the problem in a nutshell.

Another definition might read: "either the male or female division of a species . . . the sum of the structural and functional differences by which the male and female are distinguished, or the phenomena or behavior dependent on these differences." This latter definition is the better of the two. Clearly males are described as having gender. But sex is still confused with gender.

It is usually hard for men to get comfortable with opening up to the secrets of their gender. It is equally hard for women to get clear about gender issues in their lives. It's the problem of an open secret. Women have taken the lead in breaking through the secret of gender and understanding its political, economic, and social implications.

You need to understand where you stand on gender issues in your life. The following Gender IQ Test may help. It presents two lists of characteristics, one for Person A and one for Person B. Read through the lists one item at a time. If you believe that the description accurately reflects some aspect of either masculinity (Type I) or femininity (Type II) as you understand them, give yourself 1 point. Use your personal knowledge of yourself, your behavior, and your true feelings as your guiding point. If you believe that the description has nothing to do with gender as you commonly understand it, give yourself a 0. If you feel that the characteristics capture a really basic aspect of gender, give yourself a 2. Circle your score in the space provided or keep track on a separate sheet of paper. Remember: "O" if it's not relevant, "1" if it's generally typical, "2" if it's absolutely relevant. Total up your score of items checked for each list when you've finished.

Gender IQ Test

PERSON A	PERSON B
(*masculine*)	(*feminine*)

This person typically:

1. understands and prefers rationality over feeling

    0 1 2

understands and prefers feeling over rationality

    0 1 2

2. is often logical and shows more interest in things than in people

    0 1 2

is often personal and shows more interest in people than in things

    0 1 2

3. will choose to be truthful, often at the expense of being tactless

    0 1 2

will choose to be tactful even at the expense of being truthful

    0 1 2

4. is stronger in decision-making ability than in social etiquette and is likely to argue in a competitive manner to prove other people wrong

    0 1 2

is stronger in social etiquette than in decision-making ability and is likely to argue in a cooperative manner to find the common ground between people

    0 1 2

5. is brief and businesslike and may seem to be impersonal and uncaring without meaning to be

0 1 2

is friendly and sociable and may seem to care or to show concern even when they don't know the other person

0 1 2

6. is able to organize material, problems, and ideas into a logical sequence that is clear, concise, and to the point without unnecessary repetition

0 1 2

finds it difficult to know where to begin or how to organize material, problems, or ideas and may appear to be unclear, pointless, and to repeat themselves unnecessarily

0 1 2

7. will reject, discount, or ignore information that seems soft, unclear, or sentimental

0 1 2

will reject, discount, or ignore information that seems too hard, rigid, or concrete

0 1 2

8. does not express feelings well and often is uncomfortable with vulnerability

0 1 2

does not express thoughts very well and is uncomfortable expressing authority

0 1 2

9. values fairness and can reprimand people or fire employees when they've been given a chance

0 1 2

values support and finds it difficult to set limits or exercise authority over problem employees

0 1 2

10. is more problem oriented and responds to others' thoughts with the goal of being understood

0 1 2

is more people oriented and responds to others' feelings with the goal of being appreciated

0 1 2

How to interpret your score:

- *If you scored between zero and ten*, you may have responded to the statements according to a belief that men and women choose their thinking, feeling, and behaving preferences generally free of cultural influences.
- *If you scored between eleven and twenty*, you may be saying that some of these differences are attractive, but you want to retain your freedom to choose. This is the category most people likely fall into.
- *If you scored twenty-one or above*, you may have learned the cultural stereotypes about thinking men and feeling women without fully appreciating your unique abilities and priorities.

The Reality

So, how did you do? Of more importance, what were your perceptions of the items as you read them? One of my (John's) initial reactions was a vague feeling of confusion. Most of the items seemed to fit within my conception of actual, if stereotypical, differences that exist between men and women. A few seemed a little forced, while others were right on. It was those items that did not fit well or seemed forced that left me confused.

The confusion lingered, and later on was a motivating force behind a question to an astute Jungian friend: "Aren't these items really descriptions of the stereotypical ways we define masculinity and femininity in this culture?" "No," came the reply, "they're very simple descriptions of the thinking and feeling functions that exist in differing degrees in both men and women." I said to myself, "I knew that!"

And I did. But also, I didn't. A "secret" that was known, mixed in with a "secret" that was unknown.

What seems clear is that the items are, in part, an accurate reflection of attitudes that are easily recognized in men and women. There is something about these descriptions that is undeniably true. It's also true that these items were originally developed to describe the mental and psychological phenomena of thinking and feeling separate from any connotation of gender at all. This is what the confusion is about. There are two levels of reality here, not just one. It is easy to get them confused. Specifically, it is commonplace in American culture to confuse thinking with masculinity and feeling with femininity.

The issues of male and female gender—the costs, benefits, and other life-style habits of men and women—are complicated. They are also crucial to understanding the problem of codependency. In the chapters to come you'll see that all these things are related. If you are feeling a little or even very confused, then hold on. You are in the majority.

Facing the challenges that come from our insides, as opposed to fighting dragons on the outside, requires a different sort of courage than most of us are familiar with. "We have met the enemy and he (or she) is us" sets up an altogether different struggle than with the "enemy" being out "there," concrete and visible. It is like the difference between shadow boxing and sparring with a real opponent. With a real opponent the struggle can be measured and the outcome unambiguous—we win or we lose. The point is, we can keep score. Many women consider men the "bad guys." What could be clearer? For many men there is a secret self-hate that says, *"I'm a bad guy."*

How do we even make contact with a shadow opponent, much less decide on the outcome? The whole concept of "winning" doesn't make any sense if the struggle is with yourself. If you lose, you lose; if you win, some part of you still loses. This aspect of the struggle is difficult.

CHAPTER THREE

The Culture of Gender

The Parental Culture

The larger secret is about men, women, and cultures. One of the cultures involved is our *family of origin*. This is our childhood family, the intimate social context that we grew up in as preadults. It includes our parents; the values expressed in their marriage and their work; their rules, expectations, hopes, and fears for us as their children.

For most of us, this original family was a good place to grow up. It met our basic needs for security, shelter, clothing, food, and physical and psychological health. We were understood as little human beings, not little adults. Our independent thinking was encouraged, our autonomy of action respected, and our feelings acknowledged. Our world wasn't perfect by any stretch of the imagination, but on the whole, it was good enough.

Just as our family of origin provides the specific cultural context for us, our dominant social culture provides an additional, alternative "family" context for us in our development as unique people. We along with our family of origin grew up immersed in the values of our culture. This "parental" culture includes the values found on the playground, in our school, and at New Year's Eve parties. It includes all the social rules and punishments, the expectations, opportunities, and ideals that join us to our neighbors and others of our generation.

The ideas, values, and beliefs about what it is to be male don't fall out of the sky. They come to us as part of the inheritance we gain from our families of origin as well as the dominant or parental culture that influenced our parents' development in their families of origin. The values of the traditional parental cultures from the thirties, forties, and fifties are not the same as those of the sixties, seventies, and eighties. Most of us have very different ideas about what a woman can be today, compared to our parents' ideas while they were growing up.

Men's Time to Change

The social and cultural revolutions of the sixties dramatically changed the whole range of rules and roles for women, racial minorities, and youth. It opened new possibilities. Women, minorities, and youth were allowed to enjoy more of the privileges of society than they had before. It was as if the whole system of relationships between different subgroups of people in society had been discarded in favor of a less authoritative, less hierarchical, more open system.

Men, especially white men, were the ones at the top of the hierarchy. The other subgroups were somewhere below. It was as if men were standing at the top of a great pyramid of social, economic, and political privilege. And then the sixties came along and everyone on the lower levels of the pyramid moved out! The entire parental culture shifted.

Men were left hanging on to their familiar positions at work, at home, and in the public domain. Hanging on to the best of their ability because they no longer had support from below. For some time attention remained fixed on the activities of those who were busy finding new lives. Gradually, the focus of the new parental culture settled in on men, giving them the message: It's the 1990s, and it's your turn to change!

Life-style Conditioning Systems

A society as large and diverse as ours contains many different facets to the dominant parental culture. The major cultural influences center around our ethnic, religious, social, and economic backgrounds. These are components of the major parental culture, or, as we will call them, *life-style conditioning systems*. They have their greatest impact on us by their influence on our peers. Junior high (or middle) school is the great training ground for peer relationships. Every child going into junior high feels the pressure to find a peer group. The codes of dress, speech, and attitudes of these peer groups take on more importance than the codes parents set.

As individuals, we are exposed to more than one life-style conditioning system. We all recognize that the traditions of families, communities, friendship groups, and the like differ depending on whether they are, for example, urban, rural, or suburban; Protestant, Jewish, or Catholic; Anglo, African-American, or Hispanic.

These different life-style conditioning systems teach different values about what is right, wrong, moral, immoral, successful, smart, "cool," funny, and much more. They also teach us about what the possibilities are to be male and female; an egghead, a bully, a jock, a tomboy, a "bad" girl, a daddy's girl, and so forth. That is, they teach and confirm the basic rules and roles about masculinity and femininity. They give us the rules and roles we all must deal with to the best of our ability.

The urban, middle-class, white, Protestant family, the so-called average American family, is not really the average; it's just the most common. Because it is the most common it has a large influence on the life-styles of individuals from different life-style conditioning systems. The influence of television over the last forty years has brought the lifestyle values from different systems into all our homes.

The basic culture, the dominant parental culture with its homogenized life-style conditioning influences, provides an important background of values against which we judge our lives and ourselves. It provides the basis for our standards of *normality,* where normality is defined as that which is most common among those we consider our peers. The dominant parental culture is the melting pot of values that unites men and women from different subcultures into one society. The key life-style conditioning system that we are interested in for this book is the one that defines what it is to be male in American society.

Gender Awareness
An Idea Whose Time Has Come

The rules of masculinity have been discussed at some length already. Yet for many these ideas will remain difficult to grasp. All of us, in differing degrees, are reluctant to acknowledge that men have emotional needs just as women do. A hug can feel just as good to a man as it does to a woman, or even a child. The rules of masculinity are so deeply ingrained in us, in our peers, and in our culture. So we all pretend a little. We all cooperate in creating and maintaining this deception that men are somehow different: less needy, emotionally stronger, more stable, more logical, better at thinking. In a word, *emperors*.

Hopefully, the Gender IQ Test helped you gain some clarity about the existence of these rules in your own life. It is easy and common for us to think, *I don't have any rules about this male stuff in my head.* But, if you stop to think about it, you do. Everybody does. Even women. The rules exist in the images of our heroes on television and in books, as well as in the expectations of our parents and teachers. We need these images; otherwise, every generation would have to reinvent the rules and the habits of conduct that define gender roles. Think of the confusion that would create! It isn't necessary to reinvent the wheel every generation.

The major gender roles—husband or wife, mother or father, buddy or girlfriend, and worker—are the basic building blocks of society, our social relationships, and the family itself. Gender rules, like what to wear, how to walk, how to talk, what to think, and how to feel, are equally important. If we didn't have them, our society would crumble under the stress of an anything-goes mentality. The chaos of extreme individualism would render life chaotic and unmanageable.

Still, it is important to keep track of the fact that these are rules and roles that we have created. They are there to help us with the little decisions in life as well as in choosing mates, finding jobs, and learning child-rearing practices. They support our right to choose. They shouldn't dictate to us or limit our choices beyond reason.

As individuals growing up immersed in the influence of

our parental culture, we struggle with the rules and roles handed down to us. At no time is this struggle more apparent than during adolescence. As adolescents, we are just learning to form our own opinions. We are much clearer about what we don't want than what we do want. We want to be unique without being too different. As a result, adolescence is a period marked by a confusing mixture of open rebellion and herdlike conformity.

Long past adolescence, we continue to use ideas of gender roles as the key yardstick in measuring ourselves. They become part of the ideal image we hold out before ourselves, the image of what we think we are supposed to be like. Men and women both grow up following these rules and roles. Eventually we put the rebellious questioning of adolescence away and settle into the comfortable conformity of adulthood. By doing so, the stage is set for the next generation to reach adolescence and begin the cycle over again.

The Value of Masculine Gender Ideals

The value of having ideals is that they give us all something to shoot for. Ideals provide goals and standards on right and fair ways to reach those goals. Masculine gender ideals teach us about what it is to be a caring father, a loyal husband, a good friend, a dependable worker. These are questions that are critical to the survival of the family and society as a whole. How a man feels about his relationships with women, his children, his friends, and his work is central to his self-esteem and his personal happiness.

If we are to live together as a community in peace and prosperity, we need to have these common goals and rules of conduct. Problems develop when, as a culture, we begin to take the ideals of masculinity too seriously, when we forget that ideals, in any form, are abstractions. They're not real, concrete "things" that can be touched or held. An ideal, like the belief *If I just work hard enough and long enough I will find success and true happiness,* is a useful fiction. It motivates us to try the impossible and persevere against the difficult. But life doesn't always work out the way we want. It's important to know when to stop and try a different strategy.

The way our culture remembers the old West, as a place where most men wore sidearms on a daily basis, is an example of these ideals. These "memories" are kept alive by television, comic books, and movies. The message is that "real men" are tough, no-nonsense guys who are ready to risk life or take life at a moment's notice; only preachers and women didn't wear guns. The fact is that handguns were exceedingly rare! That's not how it really was. Sure, there were violent outlaws who, on occasion, required an armed posse to bring to justice. But these battles favored long guns, not handguns, as the weapon of choice. And women could use them just as well as men!

The cultural model of masculine identity has been made up from bits and pieces of history, real and imaginary, like this one. The lone knight in shining armor is a similar "memory." The parental culture's model of masculinity has been based on a selection of history's ideals. It has become a model of masculinity in its "best" and most "pure" form.

Anything that is the *best* is by definition the only one of its kind. There can be only one fastest, biggest, richest, or highest, and only one Lone Ranger. Is there any wonder that men's lives are so dominated by competition? We need some limits. The parental culture, however, doesn't recognize limits. Belief in the myth *There is no such thing as too much money* is one example of why competition instead of cooperation is such a common means of relationship between men.

Blind Commitment to Masculine Ideals Won't Work

Even the "purest" water is not 100 percent pure. Absolutely pure water is really not possible. What is the small difference worth? Not much. We will all survive with some limited level of "impurity" in our water—no one will even notice.

The same is not true of masculinity. We are all very sensitive to the slightest nuance of imperfection in our image of masculinity. We continually try to get it across perfectly. The harder a man tries to do this, however, the more failure he will experience. It can't be any other way. No one can win every time. Even business magnate Donald Trump loses!

Any man who commits to a life based on these ideals of masculinity is going to feel like a failure. The people around him will feel abused and oppressed by him. The only way to do things is his way, the "right" way, the ideal way. The man who is truly successful at this game can only end up in one place: alone with his victory. At the top of the pyramid, there is no room for anyone else to share in the glory.

It is hard to get out of this rut. The dilemma of the man with compulsive work habits, the "workaholic," is a prime example of this struggle. The success that comes with this type of compulsiveness offers some relief from the grind of constant competition. There is often an accompanying belief about the nobility of the ultimate goal that helps such a man feel special in his compulsiveness: *I'm going to be so far ahead of everybody else, I'll never have to worry about anything again.* But, the truth is, a man who works compulsively is driven by fears of not measuring up more than by any desire to get ahead.

If you are locked into the masculine ideal, you are locked into a belief system that says you are nothing until you have proved it. Idealism, of any kind, fosters a vicious extremism; you are either on the top and are okay, or you're on the bottom and are not worth counting. The world is black or white, right or wrong, with no in-between.

The tremendous sacrifices that a compulsive worker is willing to make will be his regrets of a later time. No one on his deathbed wishes he had spent just one more hour at the office. What the workaholic misses are other things: the joys of being an actively involved father to his kids, a loving husband to his wife, an enjoyable friend to his buddies.

The problem for the rest of us becomes this: How do we defend ourselves against painful feelings of not measuring up to the standards the trailblazing compulsive worker is setting? If we can't match his level of compulsiveness, does coming in second make us feel any better? We could stop comparing ourselves to others and take life as it comes. We most likely tell ourselves that this is exactly what we are doing. But, in the back of our heads, the voice of the parental culture speaks to us. Just experience a little setback. and the voice grows louder: *If I had just tried harder . . . If I had just been smarter . . . If I had just been quicker off the mark . . .*

The uncritical acceptance of the cultural model of masculinity leaves a man in the position of pretending that he is an emperor. Whatever others may think of him, he knows the truth: his life is an image. He is trapped. The only way he can defend himself against the shame of pretending to be what he is not is to deny that he is pretending. In this vicious circle, his sense of masculinity becomes defined on a negative or defensive basis. The drive to prove himself develops into a compulsive need that is similar to an addiction; it is based on denial, it is resistant to logical discussion of the "facts," it is beyond reason. Such a man becomes unreasonable. Isolated. Divorced.

CHAPTER FOUR

Final Notes on Gender

The increasing separation of work life from home life, of thinking life from feeling life, of men from women, is the less well known effect of the industrial revolution. On a psychological basis this parallels the separation of head from heart in men. The values of a dysfunctional culture become the norm, and overlap with the values of the dysfunctional family. These values, doubly reinforced, are internalized by men and produce dysfunction. The rise of a broad range of addictive and compulsive life-styles is evidence of this internal separation of parts that were meant to be connected and whole. A veil of secrecy has descended, wrapping the entire culture in a blanket of forgetfulness. We are left to ponder, *What is authentic masculinity?* The gender basis of this deception has been the key message of Part One.

At its heart, the deception is the substitution of stereotypical "male" experience in place of true self-experience. It's about how men have come to believe that a fancy suit called success—or toughness or logicalness or emotional invulnerability—is all that they need to be happy in life. This fancy suit is imaginary, but since everyone believes it, it must be real. . . . In the story of the emperor, a child sees things for what they are. A child, not yet old enough to have been thoroughly indoctrinated in ''the big secret,'' has the innocence to voice the truth. The truth is: Little boys know that it feels good to be hugged, or to share, or to give in and let someone else play. Then they get older and somehow forget.

The cultural model of masculinity is only in part a model of codependency. It is this only so far as it denies to men the soft, emotional, and vulnerable aspects of being human. This leaves man indirectly and unconsciously dependent on others—wives, secretaries, affairs—to fulfill their needs for emotional warmth and nurturance.

The truth is, a patriarchal society subordinates everyone, both men and women. The parental culture teaches little boys to forget their hearts and focus on their heads, and it teaches little girls to ignore their heads and develop their hearts. So these little boys are at risk of growing up to be men who have lost touch with their ability to feel. And these little girls are at risk of growing up to be women who are uncomfortable with the personal authority to solve their own problems. He is dependent on the freshness of her emotional vitality, while she is dependent on his ability to master the world. Together they make a good team, each codependent on the other to create a whole. And everybody pretends that it is a man's world!

Everyone pays a price for prejudice. Men gain an obvious benefit in terms of political, economic, and social power. But women gain an emotional connection to family and friends that is much closer than her mate's.

So, who is the winner here? Does it really matter? The challenge for men is to throw off the emperor's fancy clothes and put on the ordinary garb of everyday life. To do this requires men to learn values about life based not on some ideal, but on the reality of our common humanity.

The messages of the parental culture instruct men to chase after an ideal. In following these instructions too closely, men risk losing touch with their hearts. This alone is not enough to produce the debilitating condition of codependency. In Part Two you will see the effects of the parental culture in the context of dysfunctional families. Together they provide the key ingredients in the development of codependency.

PART TWO

Men in Dysfunctional Systems

> They are playing a game. They are playing at
> not playing a game. If I show them I see they
> are, I shall break the rules and they will pun-
> ish me. I must play their game, of not seeing
> I see the game.
>
> —R. D. Laing, *"Knots"*

Throughout the following discussion of dysfunctional social systems, the authors intend to develop the foundation
for a better understanding of male codependency. Some
men may come away from this material with a feeling of
being negatively labeled or somehow put down.

It should be clear that identification with any part of this
discussion doesn't translate into a need to be labeled. The
importance and benefit is not in the label. It never is. Yet in
our culture, a tremendous amount of unacknowledged male
bashing goes on through labeling.

As noted in the first chapter, there is no word to positively describe men and masculinity. We don't have a
word like *feminism*. What we do have is approximately
two hundred thousand ways to be negative about men.

There is as much contempt and prejudice against men as there is against women. It's just hard for men to see it clearly. The mystique that surrounds the emperor envelops everyone.

Sadly, many men react almost instinctively against words indicative of labels. They may carelessly disregard the possibility for help that exists if one looks past the word to the experience it points out. Typically men have strong reactions to certain words, like *addiction, chauvinist, can't, failure, impotence.*

Our intention is in no way to add another word to this list. Rather, the authors want to provide men with a more sound, balanced, and fairer perspective on themselves. Men value self-awareness. Men are capable of influencing their own self-development, if they have viable alternatives for change. Men need coping skills that are more adaptive, healthy, less rigid, designed for more than just survival.

It's true that men need to survive before they can consider any other alternative. But it's also true that life is full of potential for joy once a man has survival down and can get on to real living! The saying "Life begins at forty" speaks to this issue. It points to the reality that for most people it takes the first forty years to learn how to survive. Then we start doing what we have always wanted to do. And life turns sweet.

That is not true for everybody. The various issues that complicate men's lives today are not easy to resolve. For now, the authors' main goal is to shed light on the intertwined issues of masculinity and codependency. Many men, and not just those under forty, are torn in different directions about life: *What should I do? What should I have done? Is the present course right? What's important here? Who am I anyway?*

Men have been the focus of much public controversy and negative attention in the last thirty years. We can blame women for raising these issues, but it's not their fault. In fact, they deserve credit for raising our consciousness enough to realize problems exist. Still, many men feel they are up against the wall. They want and need someone to understand them—their problems, their pain—and to offer viable alternatives for change and growth.

Women can do the first part—they can understand—but they can't provide what men lack. Many men are using everything their personal and cultural fathers taught them as children about what men are supposed to do and be. It's just not working out anymore.

CHAPTER FIVE

Men in Dysfunctional Families

Where It All Begins

First as boys and later as young men, males launch their lives into the future by setting sail for those promising destinations that peers, parents, and culture hold out as representing their brightest potential. *What do you want to be when you grow up?* is every child's game. It's played out in children's fantasies and dreams, in sandboxes at recess, and in dialogue with adults. Often, it's a game still being played well into adulthood.

It is important for a boy's spirit of self and his zest for life to have these hopes and aspirations, even without a guarantee of them ever becoming reality. Such dreams serve the crucial purpose of giving direction to his early decision making. This is the point where he begins preparing for his career and creating the network of friendships that will stay with him throughout his life. But it's more than just what kind of job he will have, what career he will pursue, or even what kinds of friendships he will develop. Rather, it's about what kind of an individual he will be as he matures.

His hopes, dreams, aspirations, and ideas may be highly realistic or perhaps very unrealistic. They may be more myth than reality. Yet, in either case, they help him make sense of his place and potential in the world. They are guideposts that will influence the development of his common sense, his intelligence, and his favored coping skills. Together they are important tools that he will use to recreate the world he found at birth into a place of his own.

Growing up is so complex. Sometimes it feels like an adventure, other times an ordeal. Still, even when viewed retrospectively, it always seems to have been bewildering. How in the world do boys ever survive? It's amazing. The ideals, beliefs, values, goals, ambitions, social and work skills, habits of thinking and feeling that are products of growing up in different cultural, political, religious, social, and family environments all contribute to our success.

These pieces of the puzzle tend to group together into networks that the authors call "systems," because each network is organized along specific lines of authority and purpose. A man in a blue uniform standing in the middle of traffic and waving at the passing cars might be considered a lunatic. But because of the social system called the police department, he is accorded respect and his waving arm is interpreted as signals that we all obey. What of a man in a black gown and holding a gavel, or a man in a three-piece suit speaking on the steps of city hall, or a man in tights jumping up and down on a stage?

The religious, political, and cultural systems that exist in our neighborhoods, cities, and nation legitimize the actions of these individuals. When we see someone like this we know that there is more to him than just his behavior; he is acting on behalf of an entire system.

The power of these systems is in their ability to make us see what isn't actually there. The man in the blue suit waving his arms is just that, a man waving his arms. The police department isn't literally standing there behind him. But we know better. No one wants to look foolish or lose their job by being arrested. So we go along with everyone else and obey the traffic signals.

This is only the tip of the iceberg. The real strength of these systems is in the values, priorities, customs, beliefs, information, lessons, commands, and options that they represent. Whether we believe that they are trying to tell us what to do or only helping us to decide for ourselves, the influence of these invisible systems is all around us.

These systems were earlier called *life-style conditioning systems* because of their ability to shape the unfolding of a man's life. They directly and indirectly impact our development, beginning from the moment of birth. An example of this influence is our parents' decision to buy a pink or blue blanket for us. They didn't just spontaneously decide that a boy wears blue and a girl wears pink; that value was created long before our birth.

Who we are is a result of having internalized a selection from the menu of these different systems. Each human being is as complex as the life-style conditioning systems that have, in their different ways, influenced the course of a day in his life.

For many of us, the result has been a mixture of the stressful and confusing, along with the positive and successful. These interactions between the boy and his environment have developed two very important pieces of the puzzle that is a human being: a *sense of self* and a *preferred life-style* for expressing that self.

Self and Life-style

An important point to understand about the concepts of self and life-style is the nature of the relationship between them. The following exercise may help highlight the issues.

Take a coin out of your pocket and imagine it as representing an individual human being. Then imagine self and life-style as being the two sides of this single coin. Fitted together, the two sides make possible the three-dimensional reality that is a coin. Without both sides of the coin being complete and well formed, the coin itself loses its value. To the degree that either side is incomplete or damaged, the coin's or a human being's ability to function smoothly in society is diminished.

We must develop a secure sense of self and an effective lifestyle if we are to function in constructive, healthy ways in our personal and family relationships, as well as in our work and social networks. The development of self begins while we are still members of our birth or childhood family or, as it is commonly called, our family of origin.

Our family of origin is the key factor that does one of two things:

1. Provides the environment that either encourages and protects the development of self and positively shapes our life-style

or

2. inhibits and damages the self and distorts our emerging life-style.

A man's emerging self and developing life-style are intricately related. The family's unconditional love is its greatest gift. It will teach him that his self-worth is something beyond question. He will learn to love himself without shame. With the positive support and caring from his family of origin he will be in a good position to choose how to develop a healthy and well-rounded life-style. These lessons will protect him from the negative influences of his peer group.

The opposite is true if the family of origin cannot provide this caring and support. Such a family—racked by alcoholism, other drug addiction, sexual or physical abuse, emotional neglect, or abandonment—can wound a young boy as surely as a gun or knife.

A man with a wounded sense of self struggles to develop a healthy and productive life-style. Strong feelings of love, fear, hate, and other powerful reactions to the family of origin have been rolled up into a big confusing ball. When he is an adult and someone starts to get close to the inner part of him that is loving, that person runs straight into the parts that hate and fear.

The confusing internal relationships will influence how he acts in his external relationships. He will appear to others as inconsistent, shallow, and moody. Or he may appear distant, intellectual, and arbitrary. In either case he will adjust and control his behavior as best he can, trying to keep the negative aspects of himself out of the way. As a result his personal relationships, like his overall life-style, will reflect a patchwork of compromise and conflict.

With a limited or dysfunctional life-style he may be unable to make the best of the vast resources the surrounding social environment has to offer. In the face of everyday problems and disappointments, he soon runs out of options and is forced to retreat, or he becomes aggressive, controlling, defeated. He is unable to feel at home in the world of others. He never quite manages to create a world of his own.

Jim had been in therapy for almost five months. He had started with all the enthusiasm of a fish out of water, the macho reluctance to sit and be still. "You are beginning to enjoy coming in, aren't you?" the therapist commented. "Yeah, I know," he said with a smile, "Who would have believed, huh!" "You seem to relax, the tension just falls from your face," the therapist continued. "Yeah, I don't do that anywhere else," he replied, a little sheepishly. "I've grown comfortable with you too," the therapist said after a moment.

A wounded man's life-style requires extreme compromises and defensive adjustments of thinking, feeling, and behaving in an effort just to protect the self from further hurt. Over the years these adjustments of thinking, feeling, and behaving become habits. His life-style comes to reflect more of these compromises than the needs of the inner self. As his life-style becomes increasingly dominated by these adjustments, he becomes increasingly alienated from his inner self and blind to his genuine needs and the healthy support that may still be available.

Invariably, wounded men gravitate to a peer group that matches their life-styles. For the more severely wounded, this doesn't work either. So they become loners, isolated from even the possibility of support. Over a period of time, such a man's options disappear and his life potential is lost. Ultimately his spirit is shattered and with that, his life becomes truly unmanageable. He may struggle with alcoholism, other drug addiction, violence, unemployment. Barely hanging on, life may not seem worth the effort.

Dysfunctional Rules and Roles

One of the most beautiful aspects of life is how such an incredibly complicated system as a male human being can come into existence in the first place. That males can successfully get what they need from the environment to create a "fully human" individual is a continuation of this wonder. Yet, for some men, this beauty may only be a distant image or something other men have.

These are the men who have grown up in a dysfunctional family. Men of dysfunctional families find life's promise unfilled and every day to be a struggle for survival. Today dysfunctional families are an all-American, bipartisan, and nondiscriminating fact of life. They exist in every socioeconomic segment of our society. They honor every class, color, and creed.

Some general characteristics of dysfunctional families:

- a primary focus on rules and roles at the expense of people and relationships
- enforcement of rules and roles that is arbitrary and punitive
- sacrificing of individuals for the sake of the status quo

The key marker of dysfunctional families is the unbalanced focus on roles and rules instead of the legitimate needs of individuals and relationships. Every family has its share of household rules and roles. A "boy's role" is probably to carry out the garbage and cut the grass. A "girl's role" is probably to wash the dishes and help look after younger siblings. There is most likely a rule about disobeying and talking back to parents.

Why these rules and roles? Are they etched in stone somewhere? Can't girls take out the garbage and boys help care for younger siblings? Of course they can. But as a society, we have developed habitual ways of dividing chores and other family responsibilities. Over time, these habits have become part of the "normal" way the division of labor is made among family members.

Mom and Dad have their rules and roles as well. These general rules and roles can serve the best interests of individual family members by strengthening the family unit in positive and fair ways.

Roles are habitual patterns of behavior, thinking, and feeling. There are as many roles as there are individuals in any given set of circumstances. Roles serve a useful purpose. They are the building blocks out of which individuals construct their personalities. It is important to be good at something, like sports, or math, or socializing. Corresponding roles are "athlete," "student," and "cool." There is nothing wrong with this.

But, if "expertise" in that one arena is all a person is known for, then the names for the roles change. The athlete becomes a "jock" and is spoken of in the voice that communicates "dumb jock." A good student becomes an "egghead," and so forth. The point is clear; it is important to not get identified by a single role. If a guy does get labeled, there is usually a negative connotation in the subsequent name change. Even elementary school kids are quick to pick up the nuances of roles and "correctly" label them.

Healthy families know that each member's needs, wants, and abilities change. Therefore, family members are not locked into one or two roles. The transition periods between infancy and toddlerhood, childhood and adolescence, and finally adulthood are key periods of change for all families. While healthy families struggle with the demands that change in individual members brings, they do not lose their focus on the reality and specialness of the individual. As individuals change in the healthy family, so do their roles.

Not so in a dysfunctional family. Here individuals don't exist in their own right. Only roles have a reality. "You are going to do it this way because that's the way it's done." When you hear this, you know a role is being defined. In healthy families, individuals have a degree of choice in the roles they assume. Not so in dysfunctional families. "You'll do it because I said so!" The rule being spoken here is, "I'm in charge, your feelings don't count."

"He always says yes, but he never does it," she said, referring to her son Billy's procrastination about putting out the garbage. The garbage was just one of the items on her list of problem areas with Billy. "It's worse with his father," she continued, "He is more patient than I am, I guess, and Billy just takes advantage of his good nature." "You mean Billy doesn't mind his father either?" the therapist asked. "No, it's always up to me to get him to do anything," she replied with the same what-does-it-matter look she had when making her earlier comments about Billy, "You can push him and push him, and he never gets angry."

The Cost of Being a Character

What are the common roles for males in dysfunctional families? There is the "scapegoat," the guy who is constantly blamed for all the small things that go wrong in an average day. Another role is the "bad kid," the guy who appears to want credit for all the problems in his family. There is also the "good kid" who always does it right, the "mamma's boy" who hides out and doesn't participate, the "bully" who is deliberately aggressive and acts out everybody's anger, the "whiner" who struggles openly to be dependent, and so many more.

The point is that dysfunctional roles work just like adequate, healthy roles in the development of personality. They also serve as the building blocks of personality, but they lack something crucial. There is no depth to any of the "characters" that each family member is playing. Everything is superficial. What you really need, even who you really are, isn't important on a consistent basis. The only consistently safe choice is to follow the pattern; do what you have always been doing.

The cost of being safe is that men overlook and ultimately forget their deeper needs, wants, and desires. With so much denial, his life goes underground. His day-to-day experience is unpredictable, often painful, and constantly in need of change. The rigidity of the family system protects and maintains the status quo. Despite the obvious, the needed change does not occur. What possibility there is for change comes from outside the prison of a dysfunctional family. Otherwise, everyone remains stuck.

Dysfunctional family roles are rigid, and staying in line takes precedence over the natural process of discovery and expression of self. Those parts of self that have been denied expression remain undeveloped. When compared to those aspects of self that were allowed to exist, these hidden parts appear immature. These hidden parts can be the spontaneous, creative, fun-loving aspects of self. They can also be parts of self that have carried the pain, anger, resentment, guilt, and fear. These are the unacceptable parts of self, the parts the *inner critic* says no one could ever like or understand. They remain locked away.

"If this part of yourself was its own person and could talk, what would it say?" the therapist wondered to Stephan. "Nothing nice, I can tell you that," he replied quickly. He was quiet for some time and then spoke, his eyes off to the side and downcast. "I'm scared, I'm scared, I've never lived a day in my life I wasn't scared." His voice sounded small and scared. "I remember my dad holding me on the ground and punching me. I can see my mother's face over his shoulder. I can see the look on her face, screaming for him to stop." "Did he?" the therapist asked. "I don't remember," he replied.

The life-styles that men from dysfunctional families develop reflect and perpetuate all the limitations of the family roles they grew up in. These adult men leave their original families and enter the world with life-styles adapted to maintaining the status quo. They are always looking for what they missed, the piece that will make them whole—only they are looking for it in others, not in themselves. They will be happy only if they can find somebody who fills the bill, who plays the role. . . . So they gravitate to relationships that provide the opposite and complementary balance of possibilities and limitations. They are remaking the world into a place of their own, the way they were taught, the only way they know how. The circle remains unbroken, repeating itself relationship after relationship.

CHAPTER SIX

Men in Dysfunctional Culture

Cultural Roles

No man would choose the pain, confusion, exhaustion, and relationship uncertainty characteristic of dysfunctional families if he knew a more healthy and rewarding way to live. So how come he doesn't figure out a better way? What stops him?

Part of the problem for men is that there is another source of dysfunctional influence with which they must cope. This is the dominant or parental culture that instructs growing boys and men alike about how to live, love, work, and play. It is termed the parental culture because it provides, as do parents, a network of values, ideals, customs, roles, expectations, and traditions for thinking, feeling, and behaving.

If the messages from the parental culture are much the same as the dysfunctional rules from the family of origin—narrow, intolerant, disrespectful—then the maturing young man may find himself trapped without any source of support to make up for the family's missing support. Often there is hope in the parental culture through a supportive teacher, an understanding coach, or a kind uncle, if the boy can reach it. The danger is that the parental culture will merely repeat the same messages as his dysfunctional family.

The parental culture can teach us lessons about ourselves, others, and the purpose of life that we would never have gotten at home. These lessons are about commonly accepted ways to think, feel, and behave, or how we should expect others to behave. Examples include the following:

- A good husband's main job is to be a good provider.
- A man is supposed to be faithful to his word.
- Do unto others as you would have them do unto you.
- You are nothing until you have proved yourself.
- Success in life is spelled M-O-N-E-Y.
- There is no free lunch.
- Personal feelings stay inside.
- Big dogs get all the bones.

Different examples, different messages. We may not agree that this is how things should be, but we recognize that more often than not they tell the common parable of how things are in the world at large, not just in the family. Take a minute and play back the tapes of the important messages you received from the parental culture.

Johnny was sitting next to Buddy, and the coach was giving Buddy hell. Johnny's eyes were fixed on the coach's face. There wasn't much about the coach's face to notice except that his eyes were black holes, intently focused on Buddy's face. His voice was like his face, a quiet rage. He was mad, real mad, but his voice somehow didn't show it. What was he going to do to Buddy? No words went across Johnny's mind, but he knew better than to ever say "I don't want to" to the coach.

A more common way of talking about the values of our parental culture is to call them stereotypes. Insofar as they address all members of one culture, or only the men, or only middle-class Anglo men, these messages are ignoring our individual differences in favor of the group. The parental culture creates roles for its members just like a family does.

Cultural roles are different from family roles in a number of ways. First and perhaps most important, they aren't as easy to identify as family roles. Because cultural roles are so widespread, and because a culture is much bigger than the largest of families, it is hard for a man to gain the awareness that he is participating in a culturally defined role.

Family roles have become well identified in the literature of the recovery community. Roles like the family "scapegoat," the "perfect child," the "enabler," all have become known. Family roles involve, at most, only several people. Cultural roles involve all of us. The most basic cultural roles are those having to do with the gender distinctions of masculinity and femininity.

Male Cultural Roles

Remember the rules of masculinity described in the first chapter? Those rules define the cultural roles, the styles of thinking, feeling, and behaving that our culture recognizes as characteristic of men. A key rule that defines appropriate male role behavior is the one linking masculinity with thinking at the expense of feeling. Therefore, it is a man's role to be a thinker in our culture.

How does this get played out? One prominent way is expressed in many men's responses to marital conflict. A traditional husband will often approach a discussion of marital problems with a request for the "facts." He may ask for times, dates, places, and clarifications of behavior. He may continue with this rational problem-solving strategy even as his spouse is getting angrier and angrier. A traditional man will fight to stay in his head while a traditional woman will demand to be heard from her heart. The parental culture teaches men to stay rational and ignore their feelings while it teaches women to do the feeling work for two. This is fundamental to the basic American marriage contract.

Another prominent male cultural role is for men to function as workers and to identify who they are with what they do. The worker role becomes equivalent to self. It seems like boys are trained to be worker bees from birth. School continues this "education" by rewarding boys for their performance. College then evaluates that performance to select the "best and the brightest." The "b & b" boys get the jobs with the highest prestige, salaries, and status. Of course, by definition, many more men "fail" at this competition than succeed. It doesn't matter what rung of the ladder a man is on, he knows about this competition.

The stereotype is that whenever two men meet for the first time, they quickly ask, "Well, what do you do?" The conversation is likely to continue on work-related topics. This is evidence of men making contact with one another but limiting that contact to the worker role. It's like a cog in the IBM machine talking with a wheel in the GM machine. We even have the saying "He's a big wheel in_____ company." No, that's not who he *is*, it's what he *does*. When a man loses his job he doesn't disappear from the planet. Or does he?

Cultural roles, like family-based roles, are often identified by their most prominent behavioral characteristics. These characteristics for the male cultural role include:

- work ("What do you do?") as a basis for personal identity
- sex as a means of expressing and receiving intimacy
- vulnerability as weakness and something to be avoided
- competition as a primary means of male-to-male relationship
- achievement and aggression as obligations
- limits on the degree of feeling easily expressed
- limits on understanding relationship issues
- limits on direct, nurturing involvement with children

Do you recognize these brief statements as descriptions relevant to your life as a man? Use the following list of additional questions to help decide:

- Do your obligations to work usually/always take precedence over family?
- Does your wife complain about your need for sex and how closed off to her you seem?
- Do friends remark that they never can predict when you will open up with them about personal issues?
- Are you so hard that you don't have any really close male friends?
- Have you noticed within yourself a deep tiredness about how always "on the go" you are?
- Are you always clear about how you think and seldom aware of how you feel?
- Can you stay in a disagreeable conversation with friends

without getting mad, getting abstract, acquiescing, or finding an exit before there is some closure?

· Exactly how many minutes of relaxed, caring time did you spend with your children today, yesterday, last week, last year?

If answering these questions is disturbing, you are among the "silent majority" of men. *Silent* because these issues are seldom discussed among men in a truly constructive manner; they are often discussed in an angry, complaining way by women without men present. *Majority* because they reflect the cultural conditioning of men into the particular habits of thinking, feeling, and behaving that characterize traditional masculinity.

When the "training" is particularly successful, a man emerges with an emperor's image tailored to his psyche. Most men will have learned from their healthy families of origin that they still have options. They will be influenced by the parental culture's conditioning, yet they will develop other aspects of their personalities as well.

The most successful training will leave a man unable to tell the difference between himself and his image—the macho. On the other hand, when a man fails to get the training down, he often feels that he is somehow less than other men. If his family of origin doesn't provide some alternative on which to base his identity, he will develop a sense of inferiority. In the presence of other men he will always feel a sense of shame.

The Cultural Definition of Normality

What happens when a man's unique needs or aspirations lead him to cross the boundary of what's permissible within the "normal" male cultural role? What happens when he discovers around the age of forty that there is something missing from his life? Or perhaps he is recovering from an addictive life-style and notices that his Twelve Step meeting is completely different from anything else in his life. Maybe he realizes that *he* is completely different in his Twelve Step meeting.

When a man violates the standards of traditional masculine roles he is acting abnormally. An "abnormal" man faces the same problem as does the child who *still* lives in a dysfunctional family but refuses to participate in the family pathology—he is on his own. His culture will not support him or even acknowledge his efforts. It may go so far as to punish him for the violation. This punishment is called prejudice and discrimination. To wear long hair was once such a violation. Being emotional in public is still considered abnormal.

A man who drops the "image" hopes that his wife married him, not the "image." He hopes his friends will stay with him. Many men have these kinds of personal relationships. Many men have these supportive relationships and don't know it. Or they know but still can't allow their wives and friends to be supportive. Many other men don't have these relationships at all.

"You know what I think they ought to do?" the radio talk show caller was saying. "We men ought to have buttons placed on our chest, two of 'em, one that says 'macho, tough, successful,' and the other that says 'warm and sensitive.' Then they can just push whatever button they want at the moment, and we can do what they want. Save on a lot of fruitless arguments."

The message from the culture as a whole is that a man who doesn't work will be discounted as lazy. A man who values intimacy over sex has something obviously wrong with him, right? Ask any teenage boy and see what kind of response you get. Or ask a teenage girl. They both know how they are supposed to respond on questions of sex. They also know what the parental culture says on the subject: girls are supposed to say "no," and boys are *supposed* to say "yes."

Similar rules govern the experience of vulnerability—it is acceptable only under conditions of extreme duress, or under conditions of manifest, almost guaranteed support and acceptance, like those found in many Twelve Step meetings. Competition, achievement, and aggression are characteristics that men are supposed to master. If a man shuns competition, he invariably finds that he has to defend this reluctance to participate in those activities—even activities that are as innocuous as a discussion of sports or career advancement in the average corporation.

The greatest challenge to the developing man occurs when he pushes the limits of the roles from his family of origin and his parental culture in the same way and at the same time. A good example of this is in the prohibition against the expression of feelings that is common both to dysfunctional families and the parental culture's role definition of masculinity. The traditional male stereotype directs men to be tough, not to cry, not to complain, and to leave the world of feeling to women. Dysfunctional families have similar rules about feeling, especially around areas of conflict: don't say what you honestly think, don't express your true feelings, don't rock the boat, don't be your authentic self.

Women have struggled with just this same dual conflict in their efforts to claim equality of rights. Neither their families nor their parental cultures supported them in their efforts to be heard as individuals with unique needs, desires, and resources. Individual women responded to the pressures of trying to make it on their own by banding together. We now have women's groups, clubs, hospitals, and other organizations.

These roles gain their power because they define what is normal. Normal men are supposed to assume normal roles in life. The roles are not abstractions, they're real life! No one wants to be identified as abnormal. Women came together and challenged their collective parental culture, families of origin, and families of marriage to open up and expand the limiting rules and roles to include a greater range of thinking, feeling, and behaving. Many of the baby-boom generation are old enough to remember how these women were received by the media, family, and friends alike. They were attacked for betraying their children, their husbands, their own femininity, as well as the American family itself. How did they manage all this pressure, how did any of them survive? How are men going to survive?

A Healthy Normality Includes Everyone

Members of vibrant, healthy families and cultures have the flexibility to participate in many roles, depending on the appropriateness of each circumstance and the respective needs of the individual. Roles, and the rules they embody, are flexible and interchangeable. Each member can make suggestions, ask questions, assist, comfort, and support other family and cultural members. They can spend some time alone, be humorous, take charge of or assist in a family or community project, and so forth. All members are intellectually, emotionally, and physically present. Their potentials and capabilities for different roles are encouraged, explored, supported, and accepted. Each member is, in all regards, a person, not a characterization; a human being, not a robot performing a role. He is not a "real man," just a man being real.

Men from dysfunctional families, reinforced by aspects of a dysfunctional culture, learn to turn off those parts of themselves that don't fit in their assigned roles. Maybe that means they shut off their ability to be assertive, or sexual, or intelligent, or emotional, or gentle. Their daily existence becomes centered on surviving life, not living it. They lose some of their ability to be caring, to feel secure, to be competent individuals, to be committed husbands or dedicated fathers.

The guiding values of their lives and the dysfunctional rules of family and culture become one and the same. They pretend to be content if not happy. They achieve their "goals": 2.3 kids, two cars, and a home in the suburbs. Yet these men haven't a clue about who they are or what they really want from life. They can "get their jobs done," but they are simply unable to acknowledge their deeper personal needs.

"So," the therapist interrupted, "what is it that you want?" "God, ask me any question but that," Randy replied with a forced laugh that said he took the question seriously. "I've got everything, but if I knew what I wanted I wouldn't be here, would I?" His anger was readily apparent and he quickly apologized, "I didn't mean that about you, I mean, I'm not angry at you." "I know," the therapist said, "it is confusing."

Men who wear the emperor's image too dearly don't have a healthy means of meeting the legitimate needs of those they care about either. Family life, the personal, intimate, and deeper parts of life, are all managed by guess-work. Their best efforts are often just a shot in the dark. The real tragedy is that these men can live their entire life without ever actually participating in the mystery of life itself.

The key marker of dysfunctional culture is the over-balanced focus on rigid roles and arbitrary rules that constrain the thinking, feeling, and behaving of its members. What possibility there is for change and growth comes only through crisis. If the reality of dysfunctional families is as painful as it is deceptive, so is that of a dysfunctional culture. The combination of the two is deadly.

CHAPTER SEVEN

The Impact of Culture and Family

A man's sense of self develops on many levels and passes through many stages of growth. A number of important issues relate to the development of self in men who are at risk for codependency. In this chapter, the authors will integrate several dimensions of dysfunctional families and parental cultures as they relate to male experience. The authors will focus in particular on these:

- development of body image
- mirroring the real self
- expression of emotion
- difficulty asking for help
- mutuality and the need for relationship
- shame as a male problem

Development of Body Image

As an infant, our body is the vehicle by which we first experience a sense of who we are. We develop and use senses in this process of developing self. These senses include touch, smell, taste, the kinesthetic sensation of limb movement, the sense of our limb position in space, whether our stomach is full or empty, whether our bowels need to be emptied, and so forth. Through each of these senses, we grapple with a piece of the unfolding puzzle of who we are. This basic process is the foundation for all future developments of self.

Life in a dysfunctional family can have a negative impact on a growing boy, beginning at this earliest of stages. In its most severe form, this wounding of self results from the continuously high states of anxiety associated with physical, emotional, and psychological abuse, neglect, or abandonment. These events put a cast to the character of the developing man that will stay with him for all his life.

"Crack babies," those infants born addicted to crack cocaine and cared for by parents who are themselves addicted, may in twenty years show us the true depth of importance to this stage of life. For all children, the amount of attention, care, and nurturance they receive in the first eighteen to twenty-four months is crucial.

It is an exciting time for everyone when a developing boy learns to sit up, hold his bottle on his own, touch his nose or some object when his father identifies it. It may seem like the pinnacle of sophistication when he can point to the cat, but it isn't acceptable when he uses that skill to point to Dad's margarita or when he decides to pick up a doll while visiting Mother's friends. For many boys, this is where the learning not to see what they see, not to know what they know, begins.

The messages about what a boy is supposed to know about his body vary considerably in this culture. They can be at times very clear and at times very confusing. The confusion comes from other people's unpredictable reactions to male bodies. Why does Mother spend a lot of time touching her little boy, but not Father? Why is it that Sister can fall down and cry and that's okay, but the message to Brother is "big boys don't cry"? If little boys are taught to ignore the messages of their bodies, is it any wonder that men end up denying or otherwise hiding their physical vulnerability?

Of course, the truth is that little boys feel pain just like little girls do when they fall down. The truth is, being touched, hugged, and nurtured feels just as good to a boy as to a girl. But boys are taught to express their needs differently. Parents, both fathers and mothers, impart ideas about what it is to be male and female to their children through their reactions to everyday events. So the little boy who cries soon learns that what he is doing is unacceptable to his family and his culture. Or maybe it is him that is unacceptable? How do you tell the difference when you're only five?

So much training teaches boys to neglect their bodies. Sports and playground peer groups are key indoctrination agents. The so-called "male" value of not showing pain, discomfort, or physical vulnerability is communicated clearly and often. When the typical boy is hurt, he winces but clears his face before he turns back to face his peers. Whatever feelings of pain that do show through are automatically denied: "It's nothing." Later, with practice, that denial will become unconscious as he successfully anesthetizes his body against all pain.

This value spills over into his general attitude about nurturance. Whether the nurturance is about emotional or nutritional care, boys are trained to deny or otherwise be unconscious about their needs. Women are trained to do this work for them. So, just like it was in the first years of life when it was his mother who touched, held, fed, and emotionally nurtured him, now it is his girlfriend or wife's job to cook and care for his physical and emotional needs. Does the average man even know that he can do these things for himself?

All sorts of messages tell us how a male is supposed to relate to his body. It is difficult to keep them all straight. This is especially true of dysfunctional families whose messages and implied rules are often contradictory. It's tough enough growing up with a supportive family in a dysfunctional culture. How is anybody supposed to make it when the family's rules involve different reactions to the same issues?

Mirroring the Real Self

Just as body awareness is crucial to the development of a sense of self for the young boy, so is the interactional event called mirroring. Mirroring occurs every time someone, like Father, recognizes a boy's feelings, shares his excitement or his grief, or any other expression of self, and responds with acknowledgment. An acknowledging response from Father is not simply agreement, it is a communication that the boy is *visible* to Father. Father looks past the words or behavior and actually "sees" the boy himself. This kind of reaction communicates an understanding and acceptance of the boy, even if his behavior is not acceptable. It says, *I care enough about you not to confuse who you are with what you do*. By his reacting directly to the boy, Father joins and participates in the boy's experience. Father actually shares in his life. Thus, the boy learns to trust in Father.

A boy gains access to the rule-making decisions of the family by Father noticing that he is feeling something and paying attention to him as a result. The parental culture's rule that a male's pain is invisible is thereby broken. The boy comes away from such an experience knowing that he is not alone, not locked in a role. He learns that he counts. He's real people, too!

For an infant, mirroring provides the first clues that he exists as an entity in his own right. It is such a simple event, but it has profound consequences. As the infant develops through the stages of childhood, adolescence, and young adulthood, he learns to mirror others, to show others that he accurately "sees" them as they are. The need for mirroring of himself never changes. We all need confirmation that we exist, that we are valuable and connected to others.

In dysfunctional families this need is usually neglected. A fragmentation of self into parts that are visible and parts that are not to be seen results from the absence of mirroring. Dysfunctional family members, not just the males, are for the most part emotionally shut down. They are emotionally invisible. It is difficult if not impossible to respond to some other person's feelings if they are locked away in some unacceptable part. It's equally hard to respond if you have little sense of your own feelings. To be emotionally shut down means being emotionally invisible to yourself. What all human beings need is a response, an acknowledgment of their inner experience as something understood and accepted.

If the unwritten family rule is, *Men don't have feelings*, then it is safer not to expect acknowledging responses to your feelings. Because the parental culture has a similar rule, maybe it's safer to *never* expect a response from anyone. This leaves the guy feeling invisible to everyone, terribly alone, and misunderstood.

Consider what happens when men do express fear or uncertainty about their life, like, *I'm really scared I won't get the job*. These words seldom are spoken out loud. They are often spoken metaphorically or acted out in behavior. The *I'm really scared* message may be present in an angry disposition or maybe in a stomachache. The angry response, on one hand, pushes people away. It says, *I can handle this myself without your help*. The stomachache, on the other hand, may actually be a request for help and perhaps even nurturance, but only in an indirect way that preserves its deniability: *It's not the job, it's something I ate for lunch*.

The family interprets the culture's expectations about appropriate male behavior with its own unique twist. The rules of masculinity are cultural in origin, but each family finds its own way of communicating and enforcing them. Studies have shown that mothers and fathers both show less emotion to their nursery school-aged boys than they do their similarly aged girls, and those parents elicit less emotion from the boys than from the girls.

The stereotype of the adult male is someone who shows less and expects less emotion from others than do adult females. Similarly, there are jokes about bachelors who can't cook. Nationally, men use health-care services much less than do women, but they die between seven and eight years earlier. It seems as if men aren't getting the message. But, maybe the problems lie in the message itself.

Expression of Emotions

Emotions for the unhealthy family are viewed with suspicion. They may need to be repressed, avoided, situationally controlled, or internally denied. If they happen to slip out, it's safer to somehow justify them or put them off on someone or something else: "You *made* me angry!"

Emotional expression is often a sign that something is

wrong. That makes feelings unwelcome news in a dysfunctional family. A boy's spontaneous expression of feeling is often a threat to the rigidity of the dysfunctional family system because the standard roles are not capable of responding. Too much of the reality in a dysfunctional family is loaded up with pain. Some kind of compromise has been achieved to manage the painful feelings, and that compromise is defended. Acknowledgment of problems upsets the apple cart. Problems and the feelings associated with them are to be distracted from, not expressed, or at best dealt with only indirectly. Free emotional expression is a threat to the status quo of dysfunctional family systems no matter who is doing it.

Unlike the unhealthy family, the healthy family views little boys as having feelings, needs, rights, and potentials just as little girls have. Problems are for the most part openly discussed. Emotions are not something to be avoided. They are not to be controlled and denied. Father will really take the time to be involved so that he can understand. Father sees emotions as natural and acceptable, and he expresses them himself.

In healthy families, there is no picking or choosing which emotions are good or bad, moral or immoral, masculine or feminine. Emotions just are. They are a powerful, natural source of energy. Family members can ask for and receive comfort, compassion, and support—not emotional control or commands to be strong, to pull oneself together, or not to cry. The healthy family system provides consistency, flexibility, and human nurturance—to males and females.

There is no greater stereotype in the parental culture than the emotionally unexpressive man. His wife can't tell what he is feeling; his children can't tell what he is feeling; he can't even tell what he is feeling. Some of the worst male

bashing goes on around this stereotype. It often erupts in the
therapist's office with a middle-aged couple. They courted
each other based on their mutual fit to the basic gender
stereotypes. He was *strong, aggressive, always confident.*
Then with divorce in the air twenty years later those "manly" characteristics make him *domineering, controlling,* and
insensitive to the needs of others. The separation of the man
from his heart ends tragically for both of them.

> The group had been discussing their struggles with
> women for some time. Henry was among the most vocal
> and the most angry. The discussion abruptly stopped;
> then after a minute or two of silence, Henry began mak-
> ing excuses to the group for having to leave early. Instead
> of standing up to leave he turned to the window directly
> behind his seat and began to cry quietly.

Difficulty Asking for Help

Another way the parental culture's rules of masculinity
overlap the patterns of life in dysfunctional families is that
men raised in these families learn unwritten rules that being
sick, hurt, or depressed is weak and vulnerable, and therefore unmanly. "Real men" don't go to the doctor unless
they are extremely ill, preferably injured. If you are a strong
man, tough enough, then you can handle pain and the discomfort of illness without "complaining."

This form of cultural conditioning gives men another reason to disassociate from their bodies and to shut down physical awareness of themselves. This anesthesia of the body is
the very basis of men's difficulty in recognizing feeling
within themselves. If the body is numb, all feeling is muted,
perhaps to the point of being completely invisible. The parental culture's influence is so strong on this point that it

interferes with men ever recognizing that pain is a normal indicator of a problem.

Even if the pain or discomfort increases, men find themselves in a double-edged struggle:

- One side of the struggle is, *If I admit I'm sick, then I must do something about it. That may entail seeing a doctor, and that implies I'm weak, not in control of myself, not really tough enough.*
- The other side of that struggle is, *If I don't get help, I'll get sicker and more vulnerable, really helpless.*

This "conversation" is seldom spoken out loud and may not even be conscious. Still, it goes on all the time. It is clearly visible in men's behavior if not always in their words. Forgetfulness, procrastination, reluctance to take time from work or spend the money—these often disguise the struggle over being vulnerable.

One clever avenue of escape is to manipulate another family member into forcing us to see a doctor. This is usually not too hard, as women are culturally conditioned to take care of family health matters. Then, we play the part of the reluctant participant in someone else's overblown health concerns: "The wife insists I get this looked at, Doc." We negate our responsibility for ourselves while our tough-guy image is saved.

It was Mark's first session, and he looked shy and very confused. Mark, in his mid-thirties, had been married for six years. His wife had made the appointment for him. He had two children, a five-year-old son and a three-year-old daughter. Mark asked questions about other men who have sought help from a therapist. He appeared concerned that he may be seen as weak for not "handling it on his own," or that he may be sicker than most.

"Perhaps it was hard to come in," the therapist offered.

"Naw, it just took some rearranging of my schedule," he replied. "I was glad to do it."

A bigger issue is when alcohol or other drugs or addictive behaviors are involved. Alcohol is itself almost a rite of passage for adolescent males entering adulthood. Being able to "hold your beer" is a test of masculine adequacy for teenage boys unsure of how else to prove themselves with peers.

Do men drink abusively so much more than women because they need to prove themselves equal to their peers? Is the parental culture's conditioning of men a co-conspirator with their genes in creating alcoholics? Is it possible that men drink because it loosens them up, allowing them to transgress the boundaries of what is permissible for males in this culture? Specifically, does it allow them to be more emotional and accepting of their natural needs for nurturance, needs that are otherwise denied?

Or maybe abusive drinking is, in part, a self-corrective maneuver to right some gender-based wrong: "Well, I wasn't man enough for that challenge (fill in the blank), but I can still drink and show them (and myself) I'm tough enough." Or might it be to literally drown their sorrows and indirectly request the otherwise forbidden pleasure of nurturance: "Gee, honey, I'm really sorry. I won't do it again, but will you show me how much you care by forgiving me and helping me one more time?"

Drunk men can be passionately expressive at midnight, and in the morning blame it on the booze doing the talking. Or men can be directly dependent, unable to fend off caretaking, and blame it on the booze. This also provides an excuse for the traditional woman to increase her "natural" caretaking behavior. And so the dance continues.

Abusive drinking and the basic human need for nurturance and care are intertwined in a complex and confusing manner. Drinking is a very masculine behavior that in excess allows a man to be very unmasculine, that is, needy, feeling, vulnerable. Is there no other way for some men?

Mutuality and the Need for Relationship

In the early stages of infancy, interaction appears to be primarily one-way: parental care given to the child. There seems to be little in return from the infant, except his presence.

Yet as each month passes the child begins new interactions by returning smiles, hugs, and cooing. This is the beginning of the development of mutuality. Mutuality is the coordinated network of actions and reactions that confirm the commitment of each individual to the other. When someone provides leadership for others, he expects them to follow his lead. He also needs them to follow or he will likely begin to feel badly about his ability to lead. In the same way, when a man says hello to another, he wants the person to say hello back.

Mutuality is a two-way street. And it is also like a dance. When two people share information, both need for the other to acknowledge the sharing. Mutuality is needed throughout our life.

Mutuality is the harmony found in the walking together of two people who are obviously a couple. It's the "magic" in the basketball team that plays as a team and not as a collection of individuals. As adults, we need it in our personal friendships and our intimate relationships. To have a little mutuality with co-workers makes life so much nicer. It's something parents struggle to maintain with their children, especially their adolescent children.

> "I tell you what, John," his friend said, "there's nothing like it the first time he comes running up the stairs and says, 'Hi, daddy.' "

It's easy to discount something so subtle, so nearly invisible to the eye. Think about it. You spend fifteen to twenty years or more in a family where there is no provision for leadership, no arena of safety for asking questions, no acknowledgment of differences between individuals. That can be devastating. Missing this piece of life, a man can find himself after twenty years of marriage wondering, Does she *really* love me? or, Do I *really* love her?

Does the parental culture influence the development of mutuality? Without a doubt. One of the greatest enemies of mutuality is competition. It seems as if males are taught to compete almost from birth. The culture pays lip service to the ideal of "be the best you can be," but it tends to reward only those who are better than the other guy.

Success in competition is almost always measured on some sort of a ranking scale. A ranking scale lists men one after the other, top to bottom, each one "better than" the next: "You, Joe, scored 93.48. Tom, you scored 93.55. Henry, 93.57," and so forth. The clear message is that Henry is better than Tom who is better than Joe. Is that true, in any meaningful sense? Teachers in school assign grades this way. The judges at the Olympic games rate contestants this way. Intelligence tests assess applicants this way.

There is nothing wrong with this approach—in theory.

Problems arise when it becomes the dominant or maybe even the only way a guy is elevated. In real life this approach always produces one "winner" and several "losers." The cost always exceeds the benefit. It is a game no man really wins in the long term.

Many men confuse what they do with who they are, substituting a judgment of their performance as the only measure of their value as individuals. They need to win in order to feel good about themselves. This kind of competition ruins friendships. If it is brought home it destroys any possibility for mutuality in the marriage and with the kids.

There is no clearer example of how corporate ethics—competition at any cost—has come to replace a personal and moral ethic for men. Again, it is not that competition is bad. But if not checked, competition can outperform and replace cooperation. If not examined on a case-by-case basis, competition can wreck any possibility for mutuality. Competition brings many rewards. The costs of competition tend to accumulate in the form of IOUs. How does your lifestyle reflect your choices on this issue?

Choice is by definition the right to make decisions based on what we need as individuals in our own right. When a man has grown up in a dysfunctional family, he has become accustomed to filling roles within the family that meet the needs of the system. There is an absence of concern for how the system might meet his needs. When he moves out into the world of work and adult friendships, he carries this expectation of how things are going to be with him.

On the job, the expectation of having no choice leaves a man dependent on the company to tell him what to do. The more he believes himself to be independent, the less likely he will ever ask himself the key question, *Do I really want my life to run this way?* A man who never asks himself this question will continually find his self-esteem held hostage to the whims of others. He will likely be moody and angry. He may blame others for his own distress. The real problem remains his continued dependence on others to do for him what he has yet to learn to do for himself.

Choices of self are forfeited in the unexamined assumption of these typical male roles. Men, like women, are individual human beings with needs, potentials, and choices. In a patriarchal society, men also have the obligation to provide for the economic welfare of their families. It is a question of balance. That balance is as much off-center for men as it is for women. That is a hard lesson for adult children of dysfunctional families to learn. It is an equally hard lesson for men to learn about their roles in the dysfunctional aspects of culture.

Shame as a Male Problem

Sadly, for many men, growing up meant living in a dysfunctional family that failed to meet one or more basic human needs. Or they were met only on a now-and-then basis. It may be low-level but continuous conflict, or it may be continuous disorder bordering on chaos. The problems can take an infinite variety of forms. The common thread is that they are not good places to "grow kids."

These families are called *dysfunctional* because on some level, they don't work. Kids struggle on a daily basis to survive. They adapt as best they can in order to simultaneously get their needs met and to protect themselves from further trauma. They learn to compromise, to mask their true feelings, to hide their real needs. Kids growing up in dysfunctional families don't know that there is any alternative to the family life they have known.

Another important characteristic of kids from dysfunctional families is that they get confused about the difference between what they do and who they are. They don't learn to feel guilty when they do something wrong; they learn to feel shame.

A moderate amount of guilt can be a healthy control on our behavior. It helps regulate our natural selfishness and teaches us to respect others. Shame is different. Shame is completely and totally different. Shame is about feeling exposed before the world as worthless, intrinsically bad, or inadequate. Shame is not something that we do to ourselves; it is always something that happens to us *within a relationship*.

Shaming often happens inadvertently, like when Joey can't work the math problem at the board, and the teacher sits him down so that Danny can try. When Danny gets it right, everybody claps really loud, and no one remembers to say anything to Joey for his effort. Does Joey understand that the difference between himself and Danny is only about working on this one math problem, and only for today? No, not if he is from a dysfunctional family. He thinks Danny is right and therefore good, and since Joey was wrong, he must be bad. He gets quiet, lowers his eyes, and inside he feels shame.

This distinction is something fathers have to take special care for in teaching their children. Until children learn this difference, which doesn't happen until adolescence, all kids are prone to confuse the difference between their behavior and themselves as individuals. As a consequence, they blame themselves when something they are doing goes wrong. If they get yelled at for doing something wrong, sloppy, or backward, what they mistakenly hear in the reprimanding voice is that *they* are wrong, sloppy, backward, worthless, or unlovable as individuals.

No adult has learned this lesson perfectly. Every man grows into adulthood with leftover vulnerability to feel shame when he makes mistakes. The parental culture encourages this association by reinforcing the link between action and being for men: "You are what you do, Joey." Men who have internalized the culture's rules about masculinity find themselves in a lifelong struggle with shame. There is no end to it. Men from dysfunctional families are just that much more likely to grow up believing that their personal worth is limited by their level of achievement.

"I don't understand why you just didn't say you misplaced the damn invoice," Larry half yelled at Ross, his longtime employee. "We could have helped look for it."

"Yeah, I know," demurred Ross, "I didn't want to inconvenience you."

"Inconvenience me? You want inconvenience, try closing out the books without all the costs."

"Look, I'm sorry," Ross complained.

"Yeah, fine," Larry responded, waving his hand in Ross's direction, as if ridding himself of the problem.

As the years pass and successive layers of experience bury the original feelings deep below consciousness, these boys grow into men. Their lives are dominated by attempts to make up for and hide from an inner feeling of not measuring up, of self-doubt and fearfulness. At bottom, they feel worthlessness and shame. These feelings don't simply color their lives or influence certain facets of their lives—they *are* their lives.

If some trauma occurs later, especially physical abuse or

sexual assault, the tendency in these men is to remember the
abuse or assault as the cause of those feelings. This "re-
membering" gets the order of events backward. In fact the
trauma was not the cause. But it confirms those feelings in
a concrete way that the man may never have had before.
Now the guy has an explanation of why he feels so bad.

The question is, is a man likely to get anything from the
parental culture that might help him resolve these early
wounds? Hopefully so. There are numerous institutions that
are responsive to the difficulties of children from dysfunctional homes. But there are also the parental culture's values
about what a man is supposed to be and how he is to act.
That a man is not supposed to be a victim is one of those
rules. He is not supposed to complain or otherwise an-
nounce his special need for help with personal issues.

The subtle influence of the parental culture will reinforce
what the dysfunctional family dictates. Thus, he will deny
his pain, even to the extent of disassociating from his body.
He may put up endlessly with a particularly demanding job,
or he may make it demanding so that he will have to focus
intently on external problems. This way he will be too busy
to have time to look inward. The parental culture may reward him for "staying in his head" and solving these problems.

However it goes, the result is that he will never develop
the skills to accurately label his feelings, even if he should
notice them. With economic success he will appear to be a
"good catch" and will marry, father children, and to all
appearances be okay, if not actually happy.

Of course it won't last. Either his body will give out to
heart disease or his wife's "heart" will give out to years of
neglect. In the first case he may lose his life. In the second
he will lose everything that really matters to him. How

many men come in for therapy *after* the crisis in their marriage has blown up? How many men go on substituting addictive behavior for the warmth of human contact? How many men, after the work of therapy, find that shame and grief over what was lost lie at the core of their addictive life-styles? There is no greater tragedy.

"I don't know what she wants anymore. I'm tired of hearing everything I'm not. You know, work is the only place where I think what I'm doing is worthwhile anymore," raged Harry. He had come in with his wife, at her insistence, because of his drinking. She was getting more adept at expressing anger herself.

"What is important to talk about?" the therapist asked. Their heads slightly bowed, they answered with silent glares aimed at one another.

CHAPTER EIGHT

Between a Rock and a Hard Place

Stop for a minute and imagine: How does a man cope with the struggles of life after growing up in a dysfunctional family? Raised in a culture that tends to reinforce similar prohibitions and rigid role expectations for men about bodily awareness, mirroring and mutuality, emotional expression and relationship skills, what has he been trained to do?

On one level, he must already pretend that he isn't interested in those things anyway—it's not manly to be too sensitive. On another level, he has a hard time recognizing these issues in his life now because he was never allowed to admit they were happening to him in the first place. He lacks the verbal and conceptual skills necessary to handle relationship issues. He lacks the introspective skills necessary to accurately label his feelings.

"How are you feeling?" the therapist asked.

Ken looked up, made a motion with both hands that indicated he didn't know.

Ken caught the eyes of another group member long enough to invite a nervous response, "Hey, I thought something was going on with you, too."

"Look, guys, if you think something is happening, it's news to me," Ken stated. It was an honest answer.

Men who grew up in dysfunctional families also live in a culture that will punish them if they get too concerned with feelings, how relationships work, or the value of introspection. His family and his culture conspire to keep him blind and emotionally unknowing about the things that are really important in his life. He's in big trouble. He may use addictive behaviors to regulate his inner pain. He may develop a nice, pleasing life-style that ends up working better with his grandchildren than it ever did with his children or wife. He may fuse anger and violence and begin to terrorize all those who care about him, especially his wife. He may feel so hopeless and confused that he never even asks for help, even in the smallest of problems. Men, supposedly on top of the social pyramid called patriarchy, pay for their status with tears not shed, care neither given nor received, and ultimately, life unlived.

Men and Spirituality

Throughout our history as a country there has been the recognition that in order to maintain a satisfactory balance in life, it is necessary to have a firm belief in something wiser, more powerful, and greater than ourselves. The church has been telling us this for all ages. More recently, so has the recovery community. Most recently, the helping professions have begun to understand and accept this need as an integral part of psychotherapy.

The realization is that the family, our work, feel-good chemicals, food, or dangerous activity must not be allowed to become the most powerful force of life. If there is nothing greater than ourselves, then we are the greatest there is—a simple truism. Yet it contains the most terrible of delusions: the confusion of ourselves with God. The terror of this delusion underlies the awesome burden of responsibility for making all things work, on our own, all by ourselves. Isn't that a part of the John Wayne myth, and part of the emperor myth as well? Isn't that part of the general myth about what a "real man" is supposed to be?

Still, for some, the notion of spirituality is difficult to grasp—what has this got to do with men? The overwhelming reality of the human need for spirituality is evident in the fact that every culture throughout history has placed it in the center of its communal life. Spirituality is an undeniable human need, even if not proven or provable in itself. Yet our culture appears to be the first to seriously ignore spirituality in favor of disembodied enlightenment, technical advancement, and material comfort.

The recovery community has rediscovered that spirituality is necessary for the development of all areas of the self. This belief is described in different ways, sometimes as God as we understand Him or Her, or sometimes as a Higher Power. Whatever the reference, the importance this community places on spirituality remains consistent.

There are a number of ways to draw distinctions and make comparisons between "spirit" and "soul." Are these two different "things" or just two different ways of looking at the same "thing"? How does this question have relevance to the fate of men in their struggles to be more fully human?

An important assumption the authors make in this book is to identify *soul* as a potential that resides within every man. Many men are in desperate need of more potential in their life. They are stuck in a bind that has them cut off from the outer world as much as from their own inner world. The question of soul is about rebuilding the inward connections so that a connection is made to the greater mystery of the living web outside. It is a seemingly paradoxical assumption: to get outside, a man must go inside. To value the outside, a man must have access to the inner residence of *compassion*.

The First Step Is Compassion

Compassion is the first awakening of the soul. It is the possibility that "I" am like "them." *It presents the opportunity to value the self and the other as equals*. A man who has been deeply wounded with shame will respond to this opportunity as if it were an overwhelming burden, an impossibility.

Many men claim to have no feeling for their fathers. They discount his importance in their life or indict him in vague terms for having abandoned them early. Whatever their rationale, they deny his currency in their life.

Yet when encouraged to remember a time when they knew his love for them, a memory of his affection perhaps, their entire demeanor changes. To remember being loved by Father invariably provokes their own feelings of love for him—and they cry.

There are surely many feelings caught up in the encounter with this memory: anger, sadness, rage, or guilt. The common feeling for many seems to be grief—a simple sadness of what was desired and lost. In the moments after their tears have dried and the experience of grief has ebbed from their bodies, these men often experience a sense of compassion for their fathers.

They speak more honestly of their father's importance to

them. They admit to loving him. Many times they laugh about something that happened between them. These men are experiencing the soothing calmness of compassion. With compassion securely anchored for the moment, the possibility of an inner harmony and peacefulness develops. It is a quiet time, and the men often don't speak.

When remembered, this peace that "passes understanding" will provide a safe haven against the tumult and inconsistency of the outer world's reactions to us. We will survive because we have this inner space of soul that is nurturing and protective of our vulnerability. Others need not fear us either and may even find their vulnerability nurtured in our presence.

Spirituality is just this kind of energy. It is a transient experience of unconditionally loving energy—*heart energy*—that has the ability to vitalize a person's soul. It has the capacity to soothe inner wounds and quiet inner pain. It is the experience of a healing presence.

This use of the term *spirituality* also captures the other meaning of *spirit,* the incorporeal part of man, the part that is not necessarily within the body. The most important aspect of spirituality, therefore, is where a man's spirit is located. That is, where does a man place his attention in life? Where does he place his energies? The focus of his "spirit" may be external, on his work, his status, his achievements, even his wife. It may be, like the men described above, frozen in numbness and forgetfulness. In either case, it will not be available to vitalize the hollow inside, that is, his soul.

Life in a dysfunctional family works to disempower a man's spirit. It does so by demanding that his attention be focused on the arbitrary rules governing family behavior.

Consequently, his naturally deep connectedness with life and to his own inner self is broken. His outward-looking self functions to maintain appearances, to keep up the role, rather than to simply be who he naturally is. He feels powerless and trapped. He has a deep and growing emptiness within that yearns to be filled.

Whenever a man resorts to manipulation, control, dishonesty, denial, or other extremist behavior, he is in danger of creating a deceptive self. When he finds himself in the grips of those extremist behaviors that were once necessary for his survival in his chaotic and uncompromising family, he risks a further loss of his spirit and with it the potential for his recovery of soul.

The self that emerges from these contortions is accurately termed deceptive because it must put on the cloak of normalcy. It must adopt the dysfunctional family's global denial that anything of importance is seriously wrong. There is no abuse going on here! There is nobody but us happy faces in this family!

This self is deceptive because it is really a role performance masquerading as self-experience. Eventually it is about a man who has never been able to know himself as an individual separate from his behavior. It is about a man who has so confused who he is with what he does that he cannot tell the difference. In fact, there is no difference in his experience. Deprive him of his role—his job or wife—and he feels the pain of abandonment down to his core. He must maintain the deception that he is happy, secure, confident, optimistic, and so much more. His family and his culture both whisper in his ear: *Don't you believe it, the emperor is not really naked; he's never been more regally dressed!*

The Spirit in Crisis

A common way a man gets in touch with this vulnerability is to lose his wife, family, or both. Deprived of his wife and her supplies of nurturance, he feels abandoned. He feels cut loose from his moorings. Empty. Soulless. Unable to care for the self that has always been symbiotically tied to external sources of support. His work or other friends no longer have the same meaning. A profound sadness, different from grief, overwhelms him. Spirit has never been at home within this man's soul.

Not only do these men feel the loss of the relationship. On their own they feel lost. By themselves they feel incomplete. It is at this point that they begin to understand how dependent on external support they have been. A frequent comment is about how tired they feel. They realize how much energy has been invested in keeping up the status quo, controlling everything, denying everything. And with that realization comes the knowledge that they cannot access their own inner spirit in order to nurture themselves. Their deepest suffering is the pain of the inner spiritual well gone dry.

The emperor with his vanity is at last exposed: He is but a man, a normal human being, just like every other man. What a relief! Nothing can nurture the soul but the return of the spirit. It is a gift, the spirit—no charge. Its loss is the highest price men pay for their desire to sit like emperors on the tops of pyramids.

Leo sat with his men's group, listening to one guy complain about how his wife was impossible to deal with. Leo had always been one of the first to jump on the "it's no fair that I got the short end of the stick" discussion. For the first time, Leo refused the easy way out and took a step toward accepting responsibility for himself. He told the group, "I've been faced with a big decision. A decision I always knew was there and had to be made some day. I denied it at times and avoided it like the plague at other times. I ask myself, either my parents and all the institutions that taught me about life are really screwed up and I must relearn it all and I am totally screwed up, or it doesn't matter what I was taught. I've decided that it's old history. Dead history. It matters what I do with my stuff now. Today. I give all that other stuff up, the whining and blaming others. It just gets in my way. From now on it's what *I do* that counts."

PART THREE

Male Codependency: The Emperor's Image

There is a smile of love
And there is a smile of deceit
And there is a smile of smiles
In which these two smiles meet.
—William Blake

This section will address the concerns of men who struggle through life because of an explicitly codependent lifestyle. As you've read in earlier chapters, it may have seemed that the terms *codependency* and *masculinity* were equivalent and interchangeable. They often seem to function that way, but, of course, they are not the same. Still, the way the culture defines the meanings of the two terms does reflect a common ground in the daily lives of ordinary men and women.

Nothing is more important in a society than how individual men and women, as husbands and wives and mothers and fathers, relate to one another. These pair-bondings are the basic building blocks of marriage, family, and culture. They are key players in the transmission of culture from one generation to the next. It is important to check out the usefulness and validity of the information passed on.

Masculinity is defined in the parental culture as an *ideal*. This is a critical piece of the puzzle to understand. The patriarchal influence in the parental culture defines masculinity as the supreme accomplishment of humanity. Men are *obligated* to attain this ideal quality—and deny their failed attempts. Women are, of course, not even allowed to participate in this quest for supremacy. This is the prejudice of patriarchy. The culture truly believes that males are better than females. It shows this belief over and over again in its biases against women and in favor of men. We all know about this, especially women, even though we go about our daily lives as if we didn't.

The masculine ideal, like any ideal, implies that something is more than just good—it is the best there can be. Males are the best that can be! Think about it. Stop for a moment, if you are male, and imagine that *you* are the very best that can possibly be.

- Does the image fit?
- Are you comfortable?
- Or is there some part of you worried that, in fact, you may be walking down Main Street in your birthday suit? Remember the emperor!

One direct result of this idealization is the creation of stereotypic images of what men are supposed to think, feel, and act like, if they want to appear masculine. The definition of a *stereotype* is a standard belief or image that is held in common by a group or culture. It is the common belief of what qualities or characteristics appropriately define a person, place, or thing. The standard images of masculinity define the rules and roles that are allowed to men by the parental culture.

By idealizing masculinity our culture makes being a "real man" impossible, yet it is personally shameful to be shown as less. Why is being a "real man" impossible? Because any *ideal* is by definition something perfect, flawless, even divine. Who can do that number? It is shameful to fail because failure means being emasculated. If you are male and, therefore, at the top of the social pyramid, the only way to go is down, to where the females are. The land of "the weak, the wimps, and the sissies." Thus men are put in a double bind.

Because men have nowhere to go but down, they stay put. But staying put is just another name for being stuck. Women, because they start out on the bottom, have an upward option. For women, staying put is the painful and unacceptable option. That is why in stuck marriages it is the wife who comes to therapy first, and often alone.

The key point is that because gender stereotypes have not been recognized for what they are, the significance of the dysfunctional aspects of culture has been overlooked. As a result, the concept of codependency has stayed focused only on the effects of dysfunctional families. It is impossible to fully understand the power of codependency to shape life without also recognizing the importance of culture.

This failure to realize this second component of the problem of codependency is part of the reason why codependents have such trouble knowing what is normal thinking, feeling, and behaving. It is the parental culture, not the family of origin, that defines normality. The parental culture tells men that being normal means not talking about personal problems, not expressing feelings, and not admitting vulnerability in public. When men *violate* these instructions they often find themselves in immediate trouble. When they *follow* these instructions they invariably wind up in bigger trouble down the road. Is it any wonder that men are, in general, reluctant to enter psychotherapy, when they know the first question that will be asked is, "How do you feel about _____?" This is equivalent to asking the traditional man, "When do you want your grief, now or later?" That one question puts men in the worst of all dilemmas.

Growing up in a dysfunctional family creates the basic conditions for codependency. Living in a dysfunctional culture compounds the problem because it gives men a false idea of what is truly normal. This misleads men in their struggles to heal themselves. The effect is to insure that their struggle with life will be that much more complicated and frustrating.

CHAPTER NINE

Meeting the Emperor

The concept of codependency began with an implicit assumption that it was about people when, in fact, it was generally about women. That doesn't mean that the term was intended to be a synonym for femininity or with being female. It was not. But like the relationship between codependency and masculinity, there is a connection.

What follows is a list of codependent characteristics that are most commonly expressed in men. Read through the items and listen to your inner reactions. Do you see yourself here? Do you recognize the influences of the parental culture, or the dysfunctional problems from your family of origin?

A codependent man typically may:

1. *buy into a model of masculinity where his psychological, emotional, and spiritual needs are assumed as met, not wanted, or just not important.* He may function on only half of his potential but falsely claim to be fully independent, whole, and happy. As a consequence of this pretense, he is terrified of being

unmasked and will do anything to keep up the facade. Nothing is too expensive, time-consuming, or too much trouble if his pride is at stake.

2. *hear his wife say she's taking the kids and leaving, that she's tired and fed up with feeling like she is living alone.* He may think that he's dedicated his life to providing and caring for his family to the best of his ability, and now it doesn't seem like any of it counts.

3. *become a provider and protector, especially to partners who are frightened and needy,* in an attempt to vicariously fulfill his own needs for psychological closeness, emotional warmth, and spiritual security. He may confuse love and providing, and tend to love people who can't provide for or protect themselves. He is in general attracted by weakness and dependence in his life, friendship, and career relationships.

4. *have been successful and achieved advancement before others his own age,* and then realized that his kids are afraid of him and his wife is having an affair.

5. *look for the approval of older men whom he admires.* But it's a secret that he's uncomfortable acknowledging. If he pushes himself he may discover a desire to have received more of his father's time, attention, and direct expressions of care and love. He may even realize how important it is to him to be a better father to his children than his father was to him.

6. *have lost a child and feel overwhelmed with the urge to cry, but can't,* then find himself telling his wife, who is crying, that everything will be okay, there will be an opportunity to have another child.

7. *find crises at work to be the only times he finds real enthusiasm and satisfaction with his job*. Otherwise he works on automatic pilot. He may be too numb to realize how sick and tired he is of always having to compete with everyone and everything, of the constant struggle to stay on guard, of tolerating the isolation and loneliness, and of never being able to just relax without feeling tension.

8. *be attracted to emotionally spontaneous and vibrant partners*. He may not be sure why a woman is attracted to him. She will likely be the first to discover the limits of their relationship and become disappointed and resentful. He may then find himself on the defensive. The anticipated separation from this woman may feel like a looming catastrophe. When and if it happens, he may feel as if he has lost his moorings in life completely.

9. *find sports, hunting, and television dominate his life outside of work*. The power of winning imaginary challenges may seem more rewarding to him than "boring" home life. He may think of himself as having good and close friends, but none of them knows anything about how depressed and frightened he is or how long he has been that way.

10. *act as if he is superhuman, regularly finding the will to rise above others, to be stronger, tougher, more aggressive, more willing to do whatever is necessary to win*. Coming home in the evening and having a few drinks may be his habitual way of numbing the feelings of wear and tear from the day. He may believe he knows good liquor and appreciates a secret feeling of superiority over the mob who just take life as it is.

11. *have a desire to protect his wife from harm or accident, a desire that dominates other parts of their relationship.* So he may follow her to work or the store, check her mail or phone conversations, and grill her about her activities each time she comes home. He may ignore her repeated protests, getting even more suspicious and resentful as each week goes by.

12. *be acutely aware of the "right" role in any situation and be constantly comparing himself against an internal yardstick of what he should do, say, think, or feel.* He may be chronically anxious, which he passes off through humor. On the one hand, he rarely identifies his options in any situation and continually settles for far less than his share of recognition or respect. On the other hand, he seldom fails to accept the responsibility for the guilt or blame in an awkward interaction.

13. *be an extremist* and believe he must either control situations, relationships, and partners, or be controlled by them. Life is judged as either black or white, right or wrong, a man's job or a woman's place. He may not have any real friends he trusts except his wife, and she is talking about therapy, apartment hunting, and divorce.

14. *often seek mood-altering chemicals, experiences, or people, and can become addicted to the excitement of competition and success.* He believes he loves his wife, even if he has been having one affair after another for years. These behaviors help cover up the depression he suffers when he is alone with nothing to do. The constant turmoil caused by the addictive behaviors also distracts him from focusing on the pain that is at the center of his life.

15. *have lost the ability to distinguish one feeling from another*. His body may have become so anesthetized that he isn't sure he has any feelings at all. The only exception is through sex. He can't get enough sex, and his wife can't find enough reasons to avoid it.

16. *be extremely competitive*. He may regularly size up situations in order to be at the center of attention, to be the best, the brightest, the most admirable. He has never realized that everything in his life is about proving himself to others, and that he has yet to make himself feel proved.

17. *feel trapped in a deteriorating relationship he wants desperately to save*. What were once his positive attributes may now be criticized as his weaknesses— strength has become stubbornness, independence has become distance, and stability has become rigidity. His partner may request that he change in order for her to stay in the relationship. He may agree about the need for that change, but his every effort also feels like he's only doing it to please her. To top it off, she may say she doesn't want him to change if he doesn't really mean it. The situation may become unbearable. His feelings threaten to erupt, maybe ruin everything, so he often decides to redouble his efforts to stay on top and control things. The next thing he hears is their therapist telling him that his attempts to control are the real problem.

18. *realize that he can't trust anyone with his feelings because trusting seems naive and that makes him feel small, like a child.*

19. *discover that his wife is planning a long evening of intimacy that includes as much romance as sex and that he doesn't want to go home*. He suspects, rightly

so, that he'll only end up feeling awkward, embarrassed, and stupid, and will probably get angry as a way to end the evening.

20. *avoid acknowledging that he is sick until he absolutely can't deny it any longer.* Being ill may leave him feeling weak, passive, and incompetent. The pattern is always that he will protest until his partner's concern gets high enough to legitimize his acquiescence.

21. *realize that he has always idealized women.* He may have read a great deal about the women's movement and equal rights. He may have a number of good female friends with whom he can talk and no male friends at all.

Did you find yourself amid these descriptions? How many times did one of them hit home? Every man is different. No one can be characterized completely by one definition. Yet estimates range as high as 80 percent of all men in the United States identify strongly with the single description about having wanted more, much more, from their fathers during their growing-up years. What's the significance of this particular feeling? Does that mean you're codependent?

For now, the authors believe these descriptions point to the emotional core of the problems men struggle to contain. They are the parts that men hide from themselves and from each other. Fathers hide these parts of themselves from their sons as do sons from their fathers. Women in many ways expect men to keep these parts hidden as well. The difference between men in this regard is the degree to which each has been able to open up this side of himself.

CHAPTER TEN

Definitions of Male Codependency

Anne Wilson Schaef has been recognized for pioneering work on codependency in her book, *Co-Dependence: Misunderstood, Mistreated*. She describes *codependency* as a "disease that has many forms and expressions and that grows out of the systems in which we live."

Schaef identifies the underlying dynamic as a disease process of addiction. This addictive process encompasses "any substance or process we feel we have to lie about." Schaef's use of the concept *lie* along with Robert Subby's focus on the importance of *oppressive rules* parallels this book's authors' understanding of the dysfunctional aspects of the parental culture and families of origin on the development of codependency. This chapter will look at the combination of these insights to establish the basis of our understanding of the phenomenon of male codependency.

The parental culture influences the *form* that the development of codependency will take in an individual. This influence is effected through the parental culture's teaching of gender roles. This gender teaching carries the message that there are two mutually exclusive domains of thinking, feeling, and behavior, one masculine and the other feminine. These rigid rules force individuals to choose, either from "Person A" or from "Person B" (see Gender IQ test on page 40). What is important to know about these messages is, *they are lies!*

The authors hold three basic beliefs about the reality of male-type human beings on this planet.

Statement One: What it is to be male is not *limited* to some subset of overall human potential; rather, it is *equivalent* to human potential in its full majesty and mystery.

"Well," someone will say, "men don't give birth to children, only women do that." This is true, but men do have a part. Read Jerrold Shapiro's *When Men Are Pregnant*, then ask a father who has participated deeply in the experience of conception and birth: Did he not carry some part of the child in his imagination? Did he not find "phantom" pains in his belly? Was he ever troubled with his own "morning sickness"?

On a very concrete level, the world seems like it is split down the middle; something is "right" or "wrong," "good" or "bad," "left" or "right," "true" or "false," "me" or "you," "male" or "female."

On another level, a psychological level, these distinctions can be drawn another way. Instead of "either/or," the distinction can be "either/or/both." The possibility for sharing and mutuality between individuals springs from this fluidity. In every relationship there is a "me" and a "you" and an "us," all real and important. To "walk a mile in someone's shoes" speaks to this possibility. The Christian marriage ceremony speaks of the "two becoming one." All are possibilities.

The point is that males have choices about their lives,

choices they in many ways don't use, choices to enjoy more of life's wonderments: to be a worker and a father, to be analytical and emotional, to be tough and sensitive, to be a giver and a taker, fearful and brave, a sports nut and an attentive husband. Possibilities.

Statement Two: Male codependency is one of the forms codependency takes, reflecting the gender conditioning influences of the parental culture a man grew up under as much as the impact of the dysfunction in his family of origin.

The key part of Subby's definition given in the first section can be made to read as: The "systems in which we live" as men in fact perpetuate "exposure to and practice of a set of oppressive rules." The authors believe that as men living in the systems of the parental culture, and of the different ethnic, religious, political, and regional neighborhoods, we are taught lessons, given rules, and molded into roles representing the "normal man."

The addictive process is a process we feel we must be deceptive about. As such, it becomes an analogue of the ideal masculine model presented by the parental culture, a model forever beyond our personal reach. Thus, all *honest* efforts to model ourselves after this ideal must lead to frustration, disappointment, and ultimately to failure and shame—unless, of course, we pretend, or dissemble, or just plain lie about it! But a single deception to others won't work. We must also deceive ourselves. We must lie to others and we must lie to ourselves.

A simple lie won't work. To maintain the charade of being adequate to this system of ideals requires the complex lie of the "open secret" kind. The myth of the emperor parading before his subjects dressed only in his new "image'' represents such a lie. It is such a good example of this type of lie because it includes the participation of everyone, not just the emperor. The whole kingdom, like our whole culture, participates in the lie handed down from above that says that men dressed in their fancy illusions of masculinity are fully clothed.

The emperor, who represents the average man, is not guilty of a malicious lie. He has been deceived himself about the reality of human nature and relationships. His vanity—the willingness to believe that he is something special, better than the rest of us—leaves him vulnerable to the seductions of the shimmering image. The image represents the parental culture's definition of masculinity: the biggest, the best, the strongest, the whole nine yards. It represents, in a richly symbolic way, the elements of life for a man who has accepted the lessons of the parental culture without ever having examined them.

Maintaining this deception is part of the burden men carry as they move through life. Men don't buy into the lessons of the parental culture; they are seduced with the myth of masculine superiority: "Get your chance to stand at the top of the pyramid—girls need not apply!" This is exactly the message given out in grade school. For adults, this myth of superiority weaves a tale of "everyman an emperor, every home *his* castle." It is false, just as patriarchy is false, but is it powerful!

Why is it so hard for men to give up the pretense for the everyday rewards of life with family and friends? The answer is: *The emperor myth is more than a seduction; it is also a solution.* This is the key to understanding male codependency. When men have the misfortune to suffer the abuses of dysfunctional families, they respond with their best efforts to cope. Whatever it takes to survive. The strategies that males typically try are those consistent with the lessons given them by the parental culture. What are those lessons?

How many men can still remember the story of the Spartan boy who hid a squirrel (rabbit, fox, baby wolf) in his tunic before he went to school? While at school the squirrel began to claw (bite) at his stomach. The Spartan boy, true to his heritage, would not complain and died from loss of blood.

The story has been handed down in several versions, but the message is always the same: Real men don't complain, expose their vulnerability, or show feelings. And so it is with the pain of life in a dysfunctional family. The charade of the emperor gives the man one solution to the dilemma of life in a dysfunctional family: *pretend everything is fine.* The message to the young boy will remain consistent throughout his lifetime. The emperor solution will ''work'' against every type of adversity or setback. A man should redouble his efforts to withstand the pain and carry on. He should never complain or let on that he is not okay.

He should deny he even wants, much less needs, nurturance, care, affection, or any other of the basic human needs children require to prosper as adults. As an adult he will continue to deny his needs. He will value his ''independence,'' he will shy away from intimacy, he will avoid strong expression of feeling, he will not share personal history. In short, he will follow the codependency rules: don't feel, don't express, don't talk. At this point they overlap completely with the rules of masculinity.

As long as others cooperate with him to maintain the illusion of his invulnerability, he will be able to function. Each time the inner confusion and tumult threaten to erupt into his daily life, he will push them back down. He will be rewarded for his success with a fine eulogy: "He had a tough life growing up, but he never complained." The post-script might be added: "He never got any help, either." Or, "He was never really happy a day in his life."

Mike Lew, writing about the journey of men recovering from sexual abuse as children in *Victims No Longer,* says it clearly: "Men are not supposed to be victims!" By follow-ing the injunctions of the parental culture, a man will deny that he has been wounded and that he needs help. In order to continue to function, he will build a higher wall around his pain. He will refuse advice about getting some profes-sional help. He may even be admired because of his "strong character." The very solution he applies to his pain will reinforce the isolation of that pain, thus insuring that it stays frozen in time. He will honor the rules of masculinity and stay in the roles prescribed by the parental culture, even if it kills him.

Statement Three: Codependents always come in pairs, each owing allegiance to one-half of the human potential for wholeness, each needing the other to feel complete.

Codependents honor their "cultures of origin" as much as their families of origin. The dysfunctional family is the source of the trauma and pain that force an abandonment of self. The parental culture provides the directions for how males and females are supposed to handle that abandon-ment. Taken together they provide the blueprint for the phenomenon of codependency.

For the male, just as the female, the psyche will be split internally. The parental culture defines the feeling dimen-sion of life as feminine. Therefore, the rules of masculinity dictate that a male should cast off and deny the feeling side. So this part of him will go underground. To give himself the safety and nurturance he needs, the traditional male will become attracted to a woman with the complementary internal arrangement to her psyche.

This woman will have a history of dysfunctional family life experiences that parallel those in his own life. That history will heighten her vulnerability to the parental culture's rules on femininity. So, she will focus on the feeling dimension of life, nurturance and caretaking of others, and cast off the "masculine" parts of herself. Do you remember "Person A," the "masculine" items, from the Gender IQ Test? She will be attracted to a man who exemplifies all those attributes. The quid pro quo is: She will do his feeling for him, he will do her thinking for her. They are *both* codependent.

This is not the common understanding of codependency in males. Traditionally, health care experts have not made a distinction between male and female versions of codependency. The common understanding of codependency is based on what has been identified here as a "female" model. Therefore, codependency as a "caretaking" personality style or disorder emerged as the norm, for both men and women.

Many men identify themselves as codependents based on this "female" model. This is easily done because there is no biological or deep psychological connection between the culture's rules of masculinity and the realities of authentic masculinity. The standard model of codependency is based on a list of *extrinsic,* or superficial, characteristics of femininity. Extrinsic characteristics of femininity or masculinity are those qualities that have been *arbitrarily* defined by the parental culture as female or male, respectively. Part Four will develop this point and attempt to clear up any confusion the reader may be experiencing.

What is important to note here is that the female-based model of codependency underestimates the true incidence of codependency among males. The most common expression of codependency among males, the emperor model, has remained invisible. In the next chapter we will discuss three common variations of the emperor model of male codependency.

CHAPTER ELEVEN

The Emperor Solution

In the upcoming pages, three variations of the emperor model of codependency will be discussed: the macho, the average guy, and the male codependent.

Type One: The Macho

Every man has a macho part. Some men cultivate this part more than others. Some regions of our society reward men for cultivating this part more than others. Vanity is the Achilles heel of the macho. Just like the emperor, the macho male likes to appear special. Being human isn't nearly enough. He must pursue the ideal in everything he does. Whether engaged in work, sports, or barroom conversations, the macho male is dedicated to his image as a "real" man.

Of course, the macho male doesn't live up to the ideal any better than do the rest of men. *But he plays the part so intently*. He puts on the emperor "image" and wears it proudly. He may be quiet, or loud and hot-tempered in his personality. Either way, he is rigidly attached to the image of himself as an emperor. And it is just that, an image. It is an illusion that he maintains by pretense.

Macho males do just that. We lie all the time—about how in control we feel, about how invulnerable we are, about the wealth of feelings that are going on inside us. A macho male's loyalty to this model of masculinity requires him to be the center of attention, but never to reveal true vulnerability. The macho male's personality, like his behavior, is very predictable. He is operating under a set of rules that restrict the range of thinking, feeling, and behaving that he may freely express. This is the central element of Robert Subby's earlier definition of codependency. It reflects the rigid, oppressive pattern of thinking, feeling, and behaving that characterize the codependent male.

A macho male is definitely all male; just ask him. He has bought into the rigid definitions of masculine behavior, hook, line, and sinker. Notice the behavior of the people in the same room with a real macho male. They go along with his pretensions. They talk behind his back, but in front of him they go along. It would be embarrassing to point out the nakedness of his pretense. But spend much time with this guy and something else develops: everyone in his presence begins to feel oppressed.

The effects of the dysfunctional culture are most clearly seen in the split between appropriate male and female roles. For a macho male, masculinity and femininity are defined as opposite ends of a single continuum, like a yardstick, with "real" men and masculinity at one end and "real" women and femininity at the other. The more a person is to one side or the other of the continuum, the more solidly masculine or feminine he or she is.

If you measure the world according to this yardstick, you end up pegging everyone at some point. The less "male" you are, the more "female" you must be, and vice versa. But to be exclusively either male or female means you have to give up all of the characteristics of the other side. When a macho male is sizing up other men, the gender continuum looks like this.

The macho male is consistent in his assessments in that he looks at both men and women from a "male" perspective. Other men are potential adversaries and definitely competitors, so he measures them on a scale that is based on power. Women are primarily sexual objects and, therefore, are measured based on their perceived attractiveness. Neither of these ways of assessing others is based on factors intrinsic to the individual. They both are based on comparisons of physical attributes, the images or "looks" of the person.

Masculinity--Femininity

| 10 | 9 | 8 | 7 | 6 | 5 | 4 | 3 | 2 | 1 |

strong ← moderate ← weak ← sissy ← homosexual

When a macho male is sizing up women, the scale looks like this:

Masculinity--Femininity

| 10 | 9 | 8 | 7 | 6 | 5 | 4 | 3 | 2 | 1 |

lesbian → rough → handsome → pretty → beautiful

In these continuums, the authors put homosexuals and lesbians at the end of each scale, not to single out gay men and lesbians as inferior, but to realistically present the mind-set of men who hold "macho" points of view. The authors do not condone homophobia; in fact, their intent is to illustrate how this prejudice hurts both the people at whom such views are directed and the people who hold such views.

—Editor

It is important to observe the two scales in tandem. Only when the two scales are placed side by side is it apparent that the macho perspective also contains the manifest sexism of the parental culture, its patriarchy. Notice that men who measure low on the masculine dimension and women who measure low on the feminine dimension are each categorized as gay or lesbian. An effeminate male or a masculine woman is presumed to be homosexual. What could be worse, if you think like a macho?

The macho way of thinking becomes clearer when the columns from the Gender IQ Test in chapter two are placed under the two ends of this dimension. The Person A (''Masculine'') list of qualities goes on the left side of the ''sizing up other men'' continuum, and the Person B (''Feminine'') list goes on the right side of the ''sizing up women'' continuum. Connecting the two columns of the Gender IQ Test in this manner highlights the rule that the macho is living out; a person has to choose from the *extremes* of human behavior—either Person A or Person B—and there is no in-between choice. By following this rule, macho males choose one slice of the human potential and lock themselves out of everything else.

Two Versions of the Macho Type

The macho style many people think of initially is represented by the guy who is dramatic, forceful, and *very* emotionally expressive. His trademarks are an open shirt, preferably white, and a gold medallion hanging on his neck. He values exercise and has a muscular physique. He has strong opinions on people and relationships. He can be and often is quite passionate about personal issues. This type of macho male seems to have chosen characteristics from *both* extremes of the continuum.

There is a little bit of macho in every man. When a man feels that macho part of himself activated, he is in direct contact with his internalized parental culture. He is under the influence of the *idealized* rules of masculinity. We often forget that ideals are extremes. To the degree that a man follows these rules he locks himself out of his emotional center. He learns to dominate or be dominated; there is no in-between. In the extreme form of the macho, he learns to deny the real importance of self through the blind obedience to the dictates of an external entity—the parental culture.

Suppose another man, having grown up with the same degree of internalization of the parental culture's expectations, finds himself closely identified with the qualities from Person B and only weak identifications with Person A? Most likely, he will harbor a secret judgment of himself as a failure as a man. What other conclusion could he form?

He will find evidence for this internal judgment in his sensitivity, his reluctance to ruthlessly compete, his appreciation of ''feminine'' interests, and so forth. He may hide these parts of himself and study business or the law. If he follows this course, he may well appear to others as passive-aggressive, intellectual, and secretive. He may also marry a woman who identifies with this extremist perspective on life even more than himself. If so, she will appear very ''feminine'' and her job in the marriage will be to express his neglected ''feminine'' interests and energies.

Is this codependency? Certainly the first version is not, right? In the second version the passionate elements are underground. Key elements of the codependency definition are present in both cases. Each man's personality is characterized by the rigidity and oppressiveness of the rules and roles he lives under. Certainly life in relationships with these men would be narrowly defined, constricted by the extreme limits of permissible thinking, feeling, and behavior. How much true self would actually be allowed in either of these relationships?

The extremism of the traditional macho male meets the codependency definitions for rigidity, oppression, and lack of emotional honesty. In less obvious ways the same extremism is present in the second "softer" version of the macho. So is this true codependency? Where is the line between the extremist restrictions on self-expression and the real, absolute loss of self?

Type Two: The Average Guy

As discussed earlier, the influences of the parental culture's values on masculinity parallel the typical characteristics of codependency to a remarkable degree. Most men (and women) tend to misunderstand the Gender IQ Test. Most men struggle with developing the abilities listed under Person B. They get caught up in a preoccupation with work as a means to avoid the uncomfortableness of intimacy as much as a means to achieve success. Their primary outlet and source of positive esteem is centered on their performance at work. Their wives tend to see it this way also.

It is common for people to develop a split between the inner and outer presentations of self. The external image, or public self, is of as much importance to a man as it is to a woman. The qualities of the public self identify a man as being a certain type and having a particular level of status. A man's image is often imbued with pride. He may even get aggressive if the image slips a little and someone has the audacity to point it out, like his wife or a stranger at the local bar. An exaggerated male image is often identified as macho, but the difference is just a matter of degree. We can all get puffed up and louder than normal at times.

The difference is not just about putting up a front to the world. It's about *really* believing in that pretense and actively cooperating with others to maintain the pretense as an open secret. The average guy can believe in the "reality" of his image even as he knows it isn't true. He recognizes the difference between his inner or private self and the image of the public self. He doesn't have the desire or need for the level of pretense that characterizes the macho male. He knows he's no emperor. Under the right circumstances, the average guy will loosen up on the controls and reveal parts of his private self. But the rules of the game for males don't allow those circumstances to come up very often.

The standard male operating procedures tend to accomplish the switching from the public, outer image to the private, inner self only with some awkwardness and personal risk. What's really going on is that opening up involves becoming vulnerable. This, of course, is a further violation of the rules. The average guy probably doesn't understand the real problem, that he took on outside values and made them his own. The rules he is following are not as rigid. The roles are more flexible. The difference between the average guy and the macho is only one of degree.

The average male interprets the awkward feeling that accompanies vulnerability, the nervousness or shyness, as indicating inadequacy. The automatic defenses flip on, and he covers up. He may even apologize to his buddies after he catches himself. It may be okay to let the shields down with the special woman in his life, his wife or girlfriend. She is supposed to keep the specifics of his inner self a secret. It is part of her job to help keep it covered.

Stuck Between a Rock and a Hard Place

We all go around keeping our vulnerability a secret. We all know that the image is just that, an image. Still, we put a lot of energy and time into pretending that it is real and valuable. This is just doing what everybody else is doing, adapting to the special conditions of our family and the social conditions of our parental culture. We grow up and make these values our own, so completely that we can lose track of who we are without the pretense. This is typical masculine indoctrination into being just "one of the guys."

You can see how a man can find himself stuck between a rock and a hard place. The internalized values from his parental culture tell him to try harder at keeping the image intact. Those in his immediate surroundings—including those people he trusts and values the most, his friends and wife—tell him another message. The television and the political realities of his job repeat both messages. Where is he to find relief?

The question is about alternatives to the old way of doing business. Where are they? As for business itself: Is he rewarded for being open and in touch at work? Not likely. In fact, he is most likely punished if he violates the rules of having a masculine image at work. Corporate America and the values of the parental culture are very much the same. It is understandably so—being the best usually pays off, in cash!

The workplace is a key life-style conditioning system for men. It has all the major ingredients:

- a hierarchy where authority is arbitrary and based on power, not merit
- a focus on competition between individuals at the expense of cooperation

- a goal, achievement orientation, at the expense of the individual
- a value on being physically tough, intellectually rigorous, and emotionally neutral

The workplace remains essentially a man's world based on choices from the Person A column. These are all good and necessary survival skills in an unforgiving world. But to what length, under every condition, is there no end?

Survival skills are not the same as living skills. The demand of being the chief economic provider of the family requires being away from home and family for much of the day—and of the week, the month, the year, life. The structuring of the workplace in accordance with the rules of masculinity is a reality that men can ill-afford to ignore. By this structuring, the work world reinforces the splitting between the private and public selves of men. The work world becomes the arena of the public self and all that this entails.

The private self might find a place for expression safe within the confines of the family home. So very often this does not happen. Instead, the family home becomes a refuge from the rigors of the daily commute, office politics, or the factory floor. It becomes chiefly a place to recover, rest, and lick any wounds received during the day. The average guy gets to thinking that he has earned his place behind the evening paper or in front of the tube. The private self gets lost under the fatigue of maintaining the public image. With that, the private self becomes a self alone, separate from wife and family.

How many average guys end up after ten, fifteen, or twenty years on the job, a success, but also a father who doesn't really know his children? The children are now almost grown and have long since given up paying any real attention to him. And what about his wife, who, now that the kids are beginning to leave, is beginning to think the same thing? How does he deserve this? Hasn't he given his best for his family, year in and year out? How can he be an average guy, yet facing a future in a single apartment?

It happens every day. Once the average guy begins to lose perspective on what's real and what's not, once he begins to believe the pretense, he's in trouble. Early in his career, the money that success brings may grease the skids. There is always more to buy. Bigger homes, faster cars, longer vacations—the American dream almost in reach! The parental culture encourages this as well.

The Good News

The good news is that the parental culture does evolve. It may be two hundred years out of date, but it's changing. Evidence for this optimism can be found in the changes now occurring in the workplace. There is an increasing emphasis on employee health, reduced levels of hierarchy in management, more "quality circles," and other forms of bottom-to-top communication. If the workplace is still predominantly a male domain governed by a "masculine" ethic, then these changes in the structure of work relationships may be evidence of a men's movement. If it's true, as feminists have claimed, that men have refused to join in the social changes that have swept across America in the last thirty years, then maybe this is the revolution coming to men. The average guy may get some help after all.

Type Three: The Male Codependent

The key characteristic of codependency is the abandonment and loss of the natural and authentic self. This loss

occurs growing up in dysfunctional families and the ingredients are located in the parent-child relationship. The developing child suffers in the hands of an impoverished
caretaking relationship. The codependency literature has
tended to group the causes into three categories:

- the physical, emotional, sexual, or psychological abuse
  of the child
- the neglect of the child's needs for food, shelter, clothing, attention, care, and love
- the psychological enmeshment of the parent with the
  child such that the child's sense of autonomy is com-
  promised

The result is that the young boy's internal resources are
severely depleted. It is not that he is determined to play out
the conflicts of his family of origin in his adult relationships
with intimates, friends, and work; it is that he has no internal alternative to the old patterns of thinking, feeling, or
behaving. He has no sense of a healthy internal self to use
in creating alternative patterns. Where the parental culture
pushes and prods him to conform to an ideal image, his
dysfunctional family robs him of his ability to be anything
but an image.

The same factors that cause the loss of self also interfere
with the development of the interpersonal skills necessary to
create a healthy, functional life-style. The parental culture
isn't telling the codependent man anything new; he's been a
role player since he can remember.

The major loss of the man who is raised in the so-called
normal family is the draining away of his emotional self—
symbolically the loss of heart. The major loss for the man

from a dysfunctional family is not the draining of his emotional self, but the real loss of self.

This distinction is crucial to our understanding of the male codependent. It is clear that the parental culture's values about masculinity are dangerous to the "normal" male. The more successful he is in identifying himself with these values, the more out of balance, rigid, and empty he is going to be.

These same parental culture's values are even more dangerous to the man from a dysfunctional family. Every time he attempts to change his life for the better the parental culture will be there to misdirect him. If he tries to ask for help, the message will be to stop.

For every setback he suffers, he will think of himself even more strongly as a failure. He will look on his history of broken relationships as confirmation that he doesn't measure up. All the parental culture's messages about what it takes to be a successful man will tend to lead him into more investment in playing roles and honoring the rules. The harder he tries to make something of himself, the more codependent he will become. His feelings of hopelessness and helplessness are real. He is in big trouble, and there is no easy way out.

CHAPTER TWELVE

Managing the
Emperor's Image

House of Mirrors

Most everyone has had the opportunity to visit a "house of mirrors" at a county fair or amusement park. The different perspectives that the mirrors reflect are actually distortions of our physical self. It is intriguing to walk around in the rooms, each covered with curved and angled mirrors, and see the many reflections of our self-image.

Even more interesting is that someone else in the same room will see our reflection differently than we do. We can never be sure what image or reflection they see. We can move around to create just the reflection desired, checking out all the variations in the process. The other person's view changes right along with ours. To show them the image we like requires making physical adjustments until the other person recognizes what we're trying to show them. The image reflected is usually variable only in extremes, from short, fat, and compressed to tall, thin, and narrow. There is little middle ground.

This is analogous to what goes on within dysfunctional

families and between codependents. A key difference between a dysfunctional family and a house of mirrors is the motivation for adjusting behavior. In the dysfunctional family, behavior is driven by what is necessary to maintain the protective effects of denial. In the house of mirrors, the behavior is driven by the desire to experience and share a new perception of oneself.

A codependent relationship is a house of mirrors based on the motivational rules of the dysfunctional family. For a codependent, the house of mirrors can be the school, work or office, garage or construction site, the office party, tennis court, or bedroom. It's a place for performance, specifically for role performance. It's about image management.

Image Management

Codependency can be understood as a management problem not unlike that of a house of mirrors. The fun and amusement are replaced with perfectionism, obsession, and compulsion. The biggest difference is a man can't just walk out of the house. He will carry it with him wherever he goes.

In image management, the true self is unconnected to the personal and intimate interactions of everyday life. These situations are dominated by role performance. *True self* is who we really are, what we actually want from a situation, what we need from someone else, how we actually feel about things, what our concerns and problems are. We may surrender true self in order to accommodate the demands of the male role in a given set of circumstances.

The *female codependent* is more likely to read the behavior of others to discern what's tolerable to them, what will please them, what will minimize the risk of displeasing them. She performs to meet those criteria. The *male codependent* projects an image of what he would like to be seen as. He is not as concerned about the circumstances or the welfare of others. He does what he needs to do in order to be acceptable. But it's an acceptable image, not what he can do for other people, that is important to him.

The image of a pyramid is helpful in understanding this point. The social pyramid is narrow at the top and broad at the base. If the breadth of the pyramid at any given level is understood to symbolize maneuvering room, the higher up the pyramid—the more traditionally "masculine" area—the less maneuvering room there is. The rigid, macho male who may be at the top has no room to maneuver at all. His well-being depends on keeping the people below in line. He *appears* to be the one in control.

The very traditional woman who is near the bottom of the pyramid has all sorts of maneuvering room. She uses it constantly to be where she needs to be to support the desires of those above. She *appears* to be the one controlled.

Imagine the classic codependent couple. He is alcoholic, and she is "codependent." His ability to function in any sphere—work, home, family, peers—is severely limited. He can't do much of anything, except drink. Where does he invest his energy? He puts it into denying there is a problem: "I'm just fine." It is a blatant lie, a pretense that he is okay. All there is to this charade is the open secret of his alcoholism.

The "codependent" woman, by contrast, is working overtime to take care of him and the fallout within the family that comes as a result of his alcoholism. She is typically less concerned with her own image; it's his image she protects. She does whatever is necessary to be there for him. She focuses on events, behavior, and other people's feelings. He is really passive, by comparison, and focused on his image at the expense of everything else. Who is really codependent here?

The problem in male codependency is managing the image. Little changes in his sense of adequacy can result in extreme adjustments and overcompensations in his behavior. He may go to an extreme to show that he is tough, or confident, or without needs. Often, he will rehearse this routine so that he will have the performance available on command.

Another problem is failed performances. How does he interpret these events to himself? How are they viewed by others? The male who is codependent rates failed performances as the low points of his life and successful performances as the high. Neither really addresses the core of who he is. None of this contributes to his ultimate welfare. This is not healthy for him. It will not make his marriage happier or his kids more respectful of him. It may make him more successful at work, at least initially. But that is another problem. Work rewards men for their codependence— calling it loyalty or being a company man. It ends up with a man who is codependent becoming a victim of his own life-style.

Image Reflecting

Going back to the house of mirrors, remember that there are as many reflections as there are viewers. The more people involved, the more complicated the situation becomes. In general, these images take the form of variations on the theme of two images in opposition. As noted, to one side is the short, fat, and compressed; the other is the long, tall, and narrow. The distinction of there being as many images as there are viewers, spectators, or participants is important.

Some people go through the motions of relationships as if living in a psychological house of mirrors and try to manipulate what others see. This is called *image management*.

Image reflecting describes the process of how the male codependent maintains a stable image of himself. Image reflecting is the feedback he gets from the environment. The behavior of his family, wife, kids, and peers at work tells him whether his image is intact or if something is leaking out. Is there something about him that others are picking up that is potentially shameful? He adjusts his image based on these feedback loops and is assured that the image is intact if no one responds to him in unexpected ways. Then he can relax. But the first hint of criticism is a cue to refocus on his image to smooth things out.

The Wall

The key factor in developing and maintaining an image is the understanding that there are certain ways men are supposed to act under certain circumstances. The dysfunctional aspects of the parental culture and a man's family of origin are the motivation for the split between his true self and the false or *imag*-inary self. The image that is created will always be in competition with his true self. The reality that shows on the outside will always be different from the deeper reality inside.

The process of image management is done on an externalized, and thus a superficial, level. The cultural stereotypes about men—"knight in shining armor," "jerk," "wolf," among others—reflect this superficial level of reality. For the average guy, other people in his life know that the image is superficial. Its existence is a "secret" to be sure, but it's an open secret.

The secret preserves the public self from too-close scrutiny. Yet even an average guy's secretary knows that there is more to him than the image. His friends know this also, and so does his wife. Their understanding is complicated by the image: *Is this a real part of him or just more of the image?* Men often open up on such an irregular schedule, there is little predictability to it. Pushing or demanding won't work. What does work is the eruption of a crisis. This creates the intense emotional environment that draws out some real parts of the average guy.

For males who are codependent, as opposed to the average guy or the macho male, the inner self is more completely shut off behind a great inner wall. It's impossible for anyone to really know what's there, including the man himself. The crisis that opens up other men only confuses this man more. He becomes more opaque, not less. He experiences his inner self as a great unknown. He is often more perplexed by his image than anyone else who knows him. He is an enigma, even unto himself. He doesn't know much about the inner workings of people. He doesn't know how to talk about feelings. He misidentifies feeling in others. He is not particularly sensitive to the relational communication of women. But this is no denial. To deny something, it must first be known. This man struggles with never having known much about himself; this is an "unknowing," not a denial.

For some, perhaps the lucky ones, the image is never secure. It needs continuous attention, consciously or unconsciously. It must be constantly monitored, re-energized, and updated. For many people who are codependent the managing of the image comes very naturally. They may not even understand how it works, just that it does. There is always an odd sense of estrangement from life along with a feeling of being invisible to others.

Invariably, the image, the public self, is one of emotional control to the point of overcontrol. There is a dependable restraint in his behavior and a rigid or obsessive thinking style that he applies to any work, family, or personal problem.

Image management is, in fact, about control. It's about having control of oneself, one's environment, and the people in it. Otherwise, something unexpected may happen. The emperor is always afraid that his wife may say something that pierces to the heart of his pretense. And then what happens? He makes a rule that she is not supposed to ask threatening questions.

Failing that, he can always confuse the issue. He can claim some sort of imperial immunity. Or, he can challenge her sense of reality in favor of his—maybe *she* needs therapy. In some way he punishes her for intruding into and past the inner wall. What he wants most, to be understood and accepted for who he really is, is sabotaged by his need to protect himself from the unknowns of his inner self. He is so unconnected with his inner self that he doesn't really trust it. It may be, after all, some kind of horrible, unworthy, unacceptable, and ultimately shameful thing.

Life in the Squirrel Cage

The external image covers and protects the shame-based inner self from exposure. This process of covering and protecting was necessary at one time. Sometime during a man's childhood he learns to cover up in order to survive. In the case of dysfunctional families, the reasons why children learn to cover up are abuse, neglect, and enmeshment. Separate from having a history of a dysfunctional family, the influences of the parental culture also teach that it is "manly" to be vague about emotional expression. Little boys of six can already be seen to cover up their feelings in defense of their masculine esteem.

Both influences—the parental culture and the trauma-induced reactions that arise out of dysfunctional family environments—teach men to cover up and protect. As the years go by some things change and others don't. It is never okay for a boy or a man to be seen as too emotional, too caring, or too revealing of his inner self. The result is that it is normal for men to never really develop a fluid sense of themselves as emotional beings.

With these lessons learned, men miss the opportunities to develop and practice basic "emotional skills" that are so necessary to managing a successful relationship. Skills men lose include the ability to "read" the subtle nuances of another's emotional expression. They also lose the ability to communicate their own emotional reactions or needs to others. Where do the lessons lead? For many men they lead to the maintenance of what were once necessary boyhood survival skills being continued into manhood, where they cause problems in all facets of life.

At a very fundamental level, these two influences come together to trap men in a no-win set of circumstances. Emperor men have limited resources internally and limited support socially. The result is that putting on the images of the emperor saps the natural energy that is derived from being in touch with one's true inner self. The vitality and passion that were once a man's by right of birth are lost. The energy that remains is artificial and lazy. It is all expended trying to maintain the status quo and keep up the image so that nothing more is lost. It is all expended in performances. It's like being in a squirrel cage—hard work doesn't get you anywhere.

For some, the performance never becomes practiced. The male who has always known himself to be very emotional inside, and who always struggled to keep the feelings from leaking out, often doubts his ability to maintain control over his feelings. If his feelings get any momentum going, if not tightly reined in, they threaten to burst out. His emotional side is so strong he has always just barely stayed in control.

This man doesn't know how to effectively control his emotional life. He has an all-or-nothing control over his emotions. He is likely to embarrass himself if he becomes emotional because of this lack of control. It is as if he has a choice. He can yell at the top of his lungs, or he can be silent. Nothing in between. He becomes like the actor in a play or movie. Others see him acting, but they don't notice the play. And of course not. They laugh. This guy hasn't got the emperor's image down very well. That relieves the others from having to participate in *his* charade. There is nothing worse than trying to get in the act, like everybody else, and failing to pull it off. All the other pretenders know a botched performance when they see one, and are often merciless in their criticism.

The reason women keep men's secrets is because they are just as trapped in the web as men. To break it would mean exposing their investment in men being the emperor—and them the princesses. The same arbitrary rules define what it is to be masculine *and* feminine. If everybody was walking around expressing his or her feelings, how would women know what was feminine from masculine? To avoid this confusion is why the rules of masculinity and femininity are so different. Teaching these rules is the job of the parental culture. We are all so concerned with appearing masculine or feminine enough, but seldom are we concerned with just being human.

So it is that women, too, have images and image problems. The expression of emotion is central to them as well. For a female, the corresponding problem is of not being emotional enough, of appearing too cold or too rational. In a word, too *masculine*. So each partner in a relationship has an investment in the image management of the other.

He is playing masculine. She is playing feminine. He is playing masculine because she is playing feminine. She is playing feminine because he is playing masculine. . . . If he were not playing masculine, he might well be more feminine than she is—except when she is playing very feminine. If she were not playing feminine, she might well be more masculine than he is—except when he is playing very masculine. So he plays harder. And she plays softer. . . . She is stifling under the triviality of her femininity. The world is groaning beneath the terrors of his masculinity. He is playing masculine. She is playing feminine. How do we call off the game?

—Theodore Rozak and Betty Rozak
The Man/Woman Game

CHAPTER THIRTEEN

Life Problems

The Grand Deception

The keeping of secrets is a form of deception. When we as individuals keep simple secrets, they seldom last. There is always someone who intentionally or accidentally punctures the balloon or lets the cat out of the bag. Family secrets are just hard to keep. Families seem to know about each other's secrets.

When secrets are kept on the larger scale of a society, of a culture, it is because they are powerful and their exposure has major consequences. When we pretend with our wife about who we are, she knows. When our culture conditions us both to keep the same secret, we still know, but we also become anesthetized to that knowing. So we know and we don't know. The deception exists on a larger scale. It is no longer just a personal drama. It becomes a grand deception affecting the lives of everyone. We all participate in the game of keeping the secret.

The main impact of the parental culture is that emotions are inappropriately stigmatized as weak, soft, dangerous, and ultimately, unmanly. That is: "feminine." What it is to be "masculine" is deeply connected with sexism against women.

There is also a cost for men. The male must struggle to keep his inner self, the core of his emotional life, alive. Also, he must keep this struggle from showing. At least not too much. Add the influences of a dysfunctional family to this pot and stir for six or twelve or eighteen years of childhood and adolescence, and what you get is a guy who doesn't have a clue about his emotional self. He is blind to his real self. He has lost his passion for life, and he isn't likely to discover himself as long as he is under the influence of the parental culture.

He is trapped in a dual struggle: the first side is about the internal drama of dysfunctional families; the second is about the struggle to gain support and acknowledgment from the external world as a man in touch with his true self.

Life Problems

So one day a man's spouse comes up to him and asks: "How do you feel about . . . ?" Or maybe the question is in the form of an appropriately vague but alarming statement: "I don't know what's going on between us anymore." The tone of voice is melancholic, and around the edges it's also angry, fed up, or disappointed. Many men, especially men who are codependent, misconstrue feelings for thinking and respond by trying to analyze the "problem": *Maybe she needs therapy*. But the real problem is that men all too often think and rationalize themselves into ruts.

This is the typical life problem for much of middle America. It is an integral part of every codependent relationship. She wants to deal with personal issues in her comfortable style, which is feeling. He wants to deal with "problems" in his style, which is analytical and abstract. He may be accused of being insensitive and uncaring about their relationship. She may be castigated for being too dependent and insecure. As long as they focus on the other instead of themselves they will be in trouble. If they are both codependent and from dysfunctional families, they were in trouble from the beginning, literally from the time they met.

The truth is that the only thing that has changed is that the honeymoon has worn off and reality is sinking in. Because of the parental culture's rule that men should compulsively deny their emotions and women should obsessively focus on theirs, she will probably be the first to wise up. She will see that the marriage has become a squirrel cage for them both and seek to change that. Because of the bias against feeling for men, he will probably not get what's going on until much later.

As she begins working on the marriage, she may discover her dysfunctional family history. The parental culture's restricting influences on women are well known, so she will begin to wonder about what else there is to being female than what she has known. She will seek support from other women as she begins to examine some of her assumptions about being a wife and mother. She may also realize that she has never really felt that she was strong enough to be on her own. And now maybe she is. She will, as the phrase so aptly puts it, "want her own space." That line will send her husband up the wall. To him it is a code phase for divorce.

She probably doesn't know what these changes will mean for her and her marriage. But for now it will be clear; she wants it different than it has been.

Nothing moves the feet of a good emperor male more than the thought of his heart and soul going out the front door. He believes that his love for her is real, and it is. But it is also true that he desperately needs her. In fact, he is far more dependent on her than he has realized. Right now he simply needs her more than she needs him. His dependency on her emotional vitality, her nurturance, her "heart," is exposed. He appears as dependent on her as the alcoholic is on booze. Now it's cold turkey time.

The more that his life has been influenced by the trauma of dysfunctional family life, the more catastrophic the effect of her leaving will be to him. The male who is codependent is already so traumatized by inner pain and suffering that he will be unable to tell the difference between the "new" and the "old" pain.

The emperor male who is the average guy, the one who is protected only by the armor of his traditional masculinity, will also suffer. He will be confused about the origins of his pain as well. He will mourn the loss of his soulmate and the keeper of his heart. His armor really works best against external threats. It doesn't work so well against strong feelings that come from inside—not when there isn't a stage on which to strut and peacock around in front of an audience. Not when he is alone with his thoughts.

The good news is that this guy can hear the sound of his own heart crying. The bad news is that he will not understand what it says. It will be overwhelming for him. He will most likely fess up to all of his inattention and self-centeredness, his focus on work and football games, all the times he lived his life as if he didn't have to work at the relationship because she would. He will get all of this.

He will understand that he has been acting like he owned the relationship. He will regret that. But he still won't get how it all came down so suddenly. He won't understand how it is that he never got wind of the imminent danger, how he remained so clueless. He will understand that he always sort of knew about the secret. What he won't get is how it stayed a secret. The perils of an open secret. In the age of women's liberation, the emperor male's lament is, "Why didn't I realize it soon enough so that I could have done something when there was still a chance!"

The Emperor Is Dead

Open secrets are about life-style conditioning influences of the parental culture. Open secrets are complicated. The idea of a secret implies something very personal, something private and essentially painful. A secret is something that is kept from others because its exposure would be painful, embarrassing, shaming. An open secret implies something shared, something known by others. These two implicit aspects that together influence the nature of men's identities appear to be contradictory: something private but shared, something painful but "imperial," something solid and real but also superficial and false. It is time men began to integrate these disparate sides of themselves. It is time the culture gave them permission to do this work. The emperor is dead, the emperor is dead, long live the man.

PART FOUR

Life Without (Too Many) Illusions

Say what you have to say, not what you ought.
Any truth
is better than make believe.
　　　　　　　　　—Henry David Thoreau

The most salient characteristic of male codependency is, paradoxically, its invisibility. Estimates reported in *Co-Dependence: Misunderstood, Mistreated* by Anne Wilson Schaef are that as many as 96 percent of all Americans are codependent. Obviously that must include a lot of men. While case examples of men are common in many codependency books, it is reported that the overwhelming majority of the readership is female. Further, it is widely considered by codependency experts that the label of *codependency* is most often applied to women. So where are the men?

The whole issue of codependency was at one time invisible. That there could be a reason for why the spouse of an alcoholic would put up with the abuse and neglect year after year, relationship after relationship, was once unimaginable. Alcoholism was believed to be strictly a pathology of the individual. Now it's known that the codependent spouse has a role in maintaining the problem. The spouse who is codependent can use that knowledge to change his or her life for the better because a whole new level of understanding has been opened up. Yet the ''discovery'' of codependency has had little impact on the lives of most men.

The reason why male codependency has remained an ''open secret'' is because the concept of codependency has never been clearly separated from ideas about gender. What it is to be masculine or feminine has been confused with the notion of codependency. In this section, distinctions will be drawn that will help clarify the connections between gender and dysfunctional life-style patterns.

CHAPTER FOURTEEN

Codependency Types I & II

Clearing the Air

The underlying problem that complicates any attempt to understand codependency in males is the confusion between the words *masculinity* and *codependency*. The complementary confusion about codependency in females has been noticed by a number of women writers. In *Sojourner: The Women's Forum*, Bette Tallen writes, "Codependency teaches us that femininity is a pathology, and we blame ourselves for self-destructive feminine behavior. . . ." In other words, because the characteristics that have traditionally defined codependency are the same as the parental culture's idealized rules of femininity, women who have followed the rules too closely often find themselves labeled as codependent. These women are, in effect, blamed for being "too" feminine. Separating the parental culture's rules on gender from our understanding of codependency is the only way to avoid this needless and sexist pathologizing of women.

Male codependency is not a unique form of codependency that is specifically about "maleness." In fact, the term *male codependency* is a sexist term; it's male bashing. There is nothing about codependency that is *intrinsically* male or female. There is nothing genetic or biological about men or women that makes for any difference in codependency. Yet there do tend to be two distinct styles of codependency. These two styles, analogous to the two persons listed in the Gender IQ Test, usually masquerade as male and female. And, it is more common for men to express one type and women another. Why? For the same reasons most people accept the items on the Gender IQ Test as reflecting real differences between men and women. This is what the parental culture has taught us to believe.

Confusing? You bet it is! The fact is that men have as much potential to feel and be sensitive, caring individuals as do women. But the stereotype of the pragmatic man for whom the words *awkward* and *romantic* are synonymous and who habitually forgets his wedding anniversary has some truth in it. However, this truth is *not* that being awkward about romance is actually masculine. Rather, the truth is that many men simply *act* awkward when they *feel* romantic. It is a *human* characteristic to act awkward when trying to do something that no one has ever taught you how to do. The same thing is true for women. There is nothing "feminine" about how many women throw baseballs. Those women who have never been taught how to throw look, well, awkward.

The real connection between masculinity and codependency is *extrinsic*. In other words, the connection comes from the outside, from the parental culture. One of the chief features of the parental culture is that it uses an external orientation to define what a masculine or feminine life-style should look like. So men tend to develop the type of co-dependency that is marked by those characteristics defined as masculine. Because the parental culture also teaches that a man's inner self should mirror his "outer" life-style, men often practice blocking their inner feelings just as they block the expression of feelings.

Types I & II

Codependency reflects the deep dysfunctional teachings of the parental culture. Chief among these is the rule that human potential is supposed to be split in two, with one half given to men and the other half to women. Children do as they are taught. Therefore, everyone chooses between the halves. Let's examine these two types as they are commonly understood in this culture.

Codependency

TYPE I	TYPE II
selfish	pleasing
powerful	powerless
self-centered	selfless
easily angry	no anger
isolated	enmeshed
no feelings	many feelings
invulnerable	too vulnerable
strong	weak
independent	dependent
insensitive	overly sensitive
unexpressive	overly expressive

Lists of codependency characteristics often mix descriptions of how people appear to others with assumptions about what they are feeling on the inside. That is, they mix descriptions of a person's life-style with descriptions of his or her inner self. The two lists of traits, above, *describe only the outer life-style characteristics* of two types of individuals. At first glance, they may not seem to be the same as codependency traits found in other books. Many of the traditional characteristics of codependency are missing—the characteristics that describe the inner reality of codependency. Examine the list of Type II characteristics of a woman in traditional codependent terms. And are not the Type I characteristics consistent with the life-style of an alcoholic man?

These life-style characteristics don't capture the inner reality of codependency. So, the "strength" and "independence" of the alcoholic are superficial; they're only part of his *image*. Up to now, the items listed under Type II have been the primary characteristics used for describing codependency. These fit the dependent, pleasing life-style characteristics associated with the rules of femininity, so it is no wonder that many more women have been "diagnosed" as codependent than have men. This also explains how men have been left out.

Yet underneath the differences in appearance, Type I and Type II individuals may experience life in exactly the same terms. On the level of the *inner self,* these individuals may experience the turmoil of codependency in the same way: the loss, the shame, the fear of abandonment. They may experience the numbness and denial, the confusion, rigidity, and judgmental attitudes that characterize codependent inner reality.

When the internal characteristics and the outer appearances of codependency are separated, differences between the impact of the culture's gender rules and the effects of dysfunctional families also become clear. The form codependency takes is largely determined by gender conditioning; the underlying personal struggle is a product of life in a dysfunctional family. This is the first step toward establishing reliable criteria for diagnosing codependency.

The Hard Male and the Soft Male

Type I and Type II characteristics describe the forms that codependency tends to take, with Type I being the "hard" version and Type II the "soft" version. Men who have a dysfunctional family background and have experienced strict gender conditioning growing up will tend to express many Type I behaviors and few Type II behaviors. Men who have a dysfunctional family background but who have escaped most of the typical male gender conditioning will tend to express more Type II characteristics.

The same is true for women. Those who have a dysfunctional family background and have experienced strong female gender conditioning are more likely to express Type II characteristics.

Dysfunctional families are all different, each in its own way, and so are the life-style conditioning influences of the parental culture. Some men pick up a little more sensitivity than others, while some women have no problem with anger. Most men who are codependent will find they have life-style characteristics of both types, although there is usually a preponderance of one over the other.

Type I & II as they commonly appear in males.

TYPE I	TYPE II
(Hard male or man's man)	*(Soft male or "sensitive" man)*
aggressive	passive
angry	depressed
acts on others	reacts to others
controls others	controls self
to control self	to control others
competitive	uncompetitive
attacks	withdraws

These men express their masculinity in *different* ways; one is not more masculine than the other. Both of these men are male, *intrinsically* 100 percent male. Every cell in both their bodies is marked with an xy-chromosome pair. Every thought, feeling, and behavior of either of these two men is male. The inner self of each man is also male.

However, their individual life-styles, how they appear to others, are very different. The parental culture defines what is masculine; biology determines what is male. Self and life-style interact with each another throughout a man's life. But there is little relationship between what it is to be male and the characteristics the parental culture labels as masculine. The confusion between *being* male and *appearing* masculine is itself another of the legacies of the dysfunction in the parental culture. Homophobia, which is no more than a conspiracy to keep men from discovering how to care about themselves, is a prime example of this confusion: "If a man doesn't *appear* masculine, then he isn't *really* male."

If the "hard" and the "soft" men share a dysfunctional family background, they are even more alike. They are both into power and control, the first of others, the second of themselves. They use different strategies to keep control and so they look very different on the outside. Yet behind the image both types of men are scared. Both have struggled and are still struggling to find a way of living that makes sense.

They both have a hard time getting to feelings other than those on their script. These other feelings include the shame and grief of a man with a wounded sense of self. They each struggle with letting other people get to know what's going on behind the ''life-style.'' Neither of them finds it easy to emotionally support others or allow themselves to be deeply supported.

With both men, the older they are, the longer the histories of failed or empty relationships they will have trailing behind. In the face of obvious problems in their lives, they both put up the same image, the ''I'm okay'' or ''I'm handling my problems just fine'' number.

Each, in his own way, is good at turning the attention off himself to others. The aggressive guy will interpret every honest effort to talk with him about his problems as a personal challenge. He will likely respond to these efforts with personal counterattacks aimed at shaming the helper. He will restate all his abilities, accomplishments, and awards, even if he has to stretch the truth. He will puff himself up and with each step he will further isolate himself. If really pressed, he will storm out of contact. It will take a woman who is a really good Type II codependent to stay with him.

The sensitive guy who is more of the Type II will find a way not to be engaged in the first place. He will not initiate intimacy in any way. If approached—and he will attract women who are Type I codependents like a magnet—he will make excuses about his health, or remain confused about his feelings, or get legalistic about really simple matters. He will often remain unnoticed, cruising along as if he were working on his life when he isn't. All efforts to confront him with feedback about how stuck he appears will be defeated by his silence. If he has a problem with his weight, he will be found in the cafeteria instead of the gym. If he has a problem with women, he will be in a serious discussion with someone about sports. If he has a problem with feelings, he will start up a discussion about the economy as a woman begins to get closer.

These descriptions are about extremes of life-styles. Most men fall into the middle range somewhere. The crucial point is that some men do fall into one or the other extreme. To call Type I the "male" version and Type II the "female" version of codependency only perpetuates the confusion about the words *male* or *female* and *masculinity* or *femininity*. Having separated the concept of gender from that of codependency, they ought not be reunited in the unthinking use of labels. The important issue for men to understand, all men, every man, is that value exists not just in their maleness, but also in their humanity.

CHAPTER FIFTEEN

A New Definition of Codependency

Getting the Concept in Focus

The common definition of codependency has been the compulsive need to please, care for, or otherwise help others at the expense of adequately caring for oneself. A problem with this definition is that it implies an internal weakness and ignores the cultural conditions that also contribute to the development of codependency.

One result is that the concept appears to many as sexist and to denigrate the very human ability to sacrifice on behalf of others who are in need. Another problem is that the symptoms of codependency have been so loosely drawn that literally everybody qualifies for the diagnosis. Where is the value in such a concept?

There is more to the concept of codependency than this. Implicit in all understandings of codependency is the assumption that the problem is a difficulty in the relationship of two people. That is the meaning of the prefix ''co-'' in the term *codependency*. By focusing on what people share in common instead of an exclusive focus on their individual differences, the codependency concept becomes a *systemic* diagnosis. A more formal if only preliminary definition of codependency might read:

> A relationship pattern involving two individuals who are united by a mutual commitment to nurture the other's unmet and unrecognized dependency needs.

This relationship pattern is, of course, part of all intimate relationships. The question is one of degree: when does this commitment become mutually destructive? The codependency concept has brought to the surface a number of important conceptual problems and special issues that are relevant to the mental health field:

- What is the relationship between the biology of gender and the cultural conditioning of gender?
- How do the effects of gender conditioning interact with the effects of dysfunctional families?
- What language is needed to better distinguish between the external appearances the authors have called "lifestyle" and the inner psychology of the self?
- What are the key indicators that a relationship has stagnated and may be headed toward abuse, addiction, or some other breakdown?
- What can the field of marital and family therapy offer to help in unraveling the complexity of codependency?

The Problem with Patriarchy

To better understand the phenomenon of codependency it will be necessary to carefully examine the notion of patriarchy. It may be that the lasting contribution of the recovery community's focus on codependency will be just such an examination. The problem with patriarchy as it is commonly understood by many in the health care professions is that only man-the-emperor is put under the microscope. Discussions of patriarchy don't often mention its victimization of men.

The metaphor of an emperor calls up visions of grandeur, power, control, danger, pride, as well as reactions of anger, fear, resentment, secretiveness, and jealousy. But it misses the point entirely to claim that the emperor has the power to be "naked" while commanding his subjects to see "clothes." That is, to be an ordinary human being and mystify everyone into "seeing" something special. Everyone participates in the charade of the emperor's new image. This is a community act. Of course, there is power and control in this story. But the emperor is just as vulnerable as his subjects.

The story of the emperor and his image is also about narcissism. It can be seen as a metaphor for the cult of narcissism that contemporary society has created. A narcissist wears life the way the emperor wears his image, with a vain, shallow, and ultimately unrewarding pridefulness. The narcissist is a walking "open secret"— everyone knows about his vanity, but word never gets back to him. His vanity is resented, it is ignored and, often enough, it is simply tolerated until a crisis looms. Why don't people object earlier? Why does the emperor go on for so long without the critical feedback? How is it that everyone goes on for so long without the bubble bursting?

Is it possible that the narcissist in each of us conspires to keep the secret from the conscious parts of self? The story is clear that it is not some edict from the emperor that inhibits the development of awareness. Each individual is confronted in the privacy of his own mind with the challenge: *Do I choose conformity and the familiar security that it brings, or do I choose the path of truth as I see it and face the uncertainty of standing on my own?* Is it possible that the women as much as the men in the story, then and now, conspire to maintain the emperor's facade so that they may each keep theirs? Is the security that comes from conformity so irresistible that no one should be expected to stand up as an individual?

Is it possible that the patriarchal system is supported, just like the emperor, by a conspiracy of silence among men and women alike? Is it easier to blame the patriarchal system than to overthrow it? Maybe. Certainly this is not true for all men or women. Yet after all of the changes of the last thirty years, patriarchy still stands. The last of the "minorities" in society is now beginning to mobilize for change in the system. This group—men—is being attacked as it experiments with change, just as other groups were. But who better than men could reveal the emperor in all his nakedness?

The Mystery of Love

The problem is that men and women—all human beings—have at best ambivalent feelings about independence. It is simply too frightening to face the world, to face life, completely *on one's own*. It is the most daring proposition possible. The "independence" that men so proudly claim is, in part, a mask that covers up the real nakedness of men. It is easy to spot the false independence because it is so bold and prideful.

True independence is marked by humility before the awesome mystery of life as God has created it. Participation in this mystery should be satisfaction enough. To think of controlling this mystery, the arrogance of even believing it possible, is humbled by the overwhelming, bone-quaking experience with it. One does not work the mystery, as Brugh Joy, M.D., points out in his workshops; one lets the mystery work you. This is where the loneliness of our basic human condition, if imbued by the courage to reach out, is transformed into intimacy. The gap between me and you is momentarily bridged, and the experience is called love.

Bibliography

Andersen, Hans Christian. *The Emperor's New Clothes*. Translated by Naomi Lewis. New York: Simon & Schuster.

Benderly, Beryl. *The Myth of Two Minds*. New York: Doubleday, 1987.

Blake, William. "The Smile." From the Pickering manuscript in *The Complete Poetry and Prose of William Blake*. Edited by David V. Erdman. Berkeley, Calif.: University of California Press.

Cleary, Paul. "Gender Differences in Stress-Related Disorders." In *Gender and Stress,* edited by Rosalind C. Barnett, Losi Biener, and Grace K. Baruch. New York: Free Press, 1987.

Donne, John. "Devotions upon Emergent Occasions." In *The Complete English Poems of John Donne,* edited by A. J. Smith. Penguin Books.

Farrell, Warren. *Why Men Are the Way They Are*. New York: McGraw-Hill, 1986.

Laing, R. D. *Knots*. New York: Random House, 1972.

Lew, Mike. *Victims No Longer*. New York: Nevraumont, 1988.

Rozak, Theodore and Betty Rozak. ''The Man/Woman Game.'' In *Challenge of the Heart: Love, Sex, and Intimacy in Changing Times,* edited by John Welwood. Boston: Shambhala, 1985.

Schaef, Anne Wilson. *Co-Dependence: Misunderstood/Mistreated*. San Francisco: Harper San Francisco, 1986.

Subby, Robert. *Lost in the Shuffle*. Deerfield Beach, Fla.: Health Communications, 1987.

Thoreau, Henry David. *Walden*. New York: Doubleday, 1960.

About the Authors

John Hough, Ph.D., is a psychotherapist in Houston, Texas, where he specializes in the treatment of men and in male psychology. He holds a doctorate in psychology and trained extensively in VA hospitals where his interest in men's issues developed. He has developed a gender-sensitive model of inpatient treatment for men with co-dependency. He continues to write on the subject of male psychology and psychotherapy. He is a member of the Men's Health Network, a private practice association that specializes in therapy and educational services for men and their families.

Marshall Hardy, Ph.D., CADAC, has extensive experience working with adult male children of dysfunctional families, male codependents, and men with post-traumatic stress. A certified alcoholism and drug-abuse counselor with a doctorate in counseling psychology, he has been nationally recognized for his consultation and training contributions to treatment and employee assistance programs. He pioneered the first Male CoDA (Codependents Anonymous) meetings and T.R.A.C. men's groups (for men in Transition, Recovery Adjustment, and Codependency). Currently he is president of Hardy and Associates and executive director of a men's resource center.